Equitable and Inclusive Teaching for Diverse Learners With Disabilities

Equitable and Inclusive Teaching for Diverse Learners With Disabilities

A Bibliography-Driven Approach

Socorro G. Herrera
Diane Rodríguez
Robin M. Cabral
Melissa A. Holmes

Foreword by Alfredo J. Artiles

TEACHERS COLLEGE PRESS

TEACHERS COLLEGE | COLUMBIA UNIVERSITY

NEW YORK AND LONDON

Dr. Julia Rosa Lopez-Emslie and Leonard Baca, I dedicate this work to you. Thank you for challenging me to always question, advocate, and be present to the rights of families and students. Forever, grateful.

—Socorro Herrera

For Benjamin L: You are my light and inspiration.

—Diane Rodríguez

For Uncle Andy

—Robin Cabral

For Benjamin, Hannah, and Nicholas: May you each find joy and inspire others with your curiosity, creativity, and unique gifts.

—Melissa Holmes

Published by Teachers College Press®, 1234 Amsterdam Avenue, New York, NY 10027

Copyright © 2023 by Teachers College, Columbia University

All front cover photos by Reinaldo Antonio Martinez

Library of Congress Cataloging-in-Publication Data is available at loc.gov

ISBN 978-0-8077-6800-6 (paper)
ISBN 978-0-8077-6801-3 (hardcover)
ISBN 978-0-8077-8155-5 (ebook)

Printed on acid-free paper
Manufactured in the United States of America

Contents

Contents

Foreword

A distinctive feature of the U.S. population has been and continues to be its immense diversity. This is most noticeable in the school-age population, with a growing presence of students of color in urban, suburban, and rural spaces. Historical evidence suggests the country's diversity has been a defining feature of national identity and a productive engine of creativity and innovation. For instance, diversity is a distinguishing feature of the immigration experience that has been historically characterized by upward mobility and substantial contributions to the economy (Abramitzky & Boustan, 2022). Diversity is also a key element of the creative class that is reshaping U.S. society (Florida, 2019). At the same time, the notion of diversity has been historically used to stigmatize, segregate, and maintain inequality. Indeed, there is no shortage of reports in the social sciences in which diversity is imbricated with inequality, disorder, and crisis. Reports on crime, health inequities, low educational performance, injustices in labor and the economy, and so forth often note how "diverse" individuals and groups are disproportionately affected. Thus, the term "diverse" is loaded with contradictory meanings—a source of pride and accomplishment, a marker of disadvantage and stigma.

In general and special education, "diverse" tends to be used as a racial codeword for non-white students. It is typically used as a proxy for racialized and ethnic minoritized students. A popular variant of the term is "culturally diverse." Again, the implied targets are African American, Latinx, Asian American, and Native American groups. Yet, the term "culturally and linguistically diverse" covers the same groups but adds dual language or multilingual learners. The common denominator in these uses is the notion of "diverse." In all uses, "othering" is at work. It is shorthand to describe groups that deviate from the assumed norm—i.e., white middle class. In all uses, the implicit message is one of deficits—i.e., these are students who are characterized for *what they are not* (not white) and embody deficits that need fixing (Artiles, 2022). In a perverse turn, the term "diverse" and its variants are invested with a veil of benevolence since the presumed essence of such groups—deficits—will be repaired by a system built on and sustained by colorblind knowledge and practices (Artiles, 2022). Indeed, scholars have documented for decades these epistemological practices (Artiles et al., 1997; Bonilla-Silva & Baiocchi, 2012; Stevens, 2022).

In this volume, *Equitable and Inclusive Teaching for Diverse Learners with Disabilities: A Biography Driven Approach*, Herrera, Rodriguez, Cabral, and Holmes wrestle with these ambiguities when naming and describing students. They call attention to the deficit underpinnings of such traditional descriptors and advance an asset-oriented approach. Their target is a distinctive intersectional group, "diverse students with disabilities." This is a unique, often neglected population in which race, ethnicity, language, and ability differences intermingle. Research about the experiences and needs of this population, particularly grounded in intersectional perspectives, is scarce (Artiles, 2013; Tefera & Artiles, 2023). The focus on the intersections of disability with language is urgent, in light of the growing presence of multilingual students in schools and pervasive misunderstandings about this population. Consider a few facts:

- **Heterogeneity**
  - » "Bilingualism in the early years (birth to age 8) is found largely among children in immigrant families, the majority of whom are U.S. citizens" (Castro et al., 2021, p. 6).

> » ". . . there are also bilinguals among children of U.S. born heritage language speakers (second generation and above) and children in indigenous families" (Castro et al., 2021, p. 6).
> » "Bilingual children are a third (32%) of the US child population ages 0–8 and constitute a higher percentage in some states: 60% in California and 49% in Texas and New Mexico" (Castro et al., 2021, p. 6).
> » Dual language learners with disabilities "make up about 9 percent of the [dual language/multilingual] population and 8 percent of students with disabilities, yet these small percentages represent more than 350,000 children" (NASEM, 2017, p. 351).
> » The largest language group is Spanish with representation from over 20 nations (62%), followed by Chinese (4.7%; including Mandarin, Cantonese, and others), Native American languages (4.3%), Tagalog (2.7%), and Vietnamese (2.3%) (Castro et al., 2021).
> » "Language competence varies considerably among dual language learners. Multiple social and cultural factors—including parents' immigrant generational status and years in the United States, socioeconomic status, exposures to the risks of poverty, the perceived status of the home language in the community, and neighborhood resources—may help explain this variation" (NASEM, 2017, pp. 3–4).
> » Bilingual individuals "are likely to reap benefits in cognitive, social, and emotional development and may also be protected from brain decline at older ages" (NASEM, 2017, pp. 1–2).

- **Misunderstandings**
  > » Emergent bilinguals belong to multiple cultural, racial, and ethnic groups in which developmental norms and expectations, child rearing customs, and learning practices differ from monolingual Eurocentric models. Yet, many U.S. studies with multilingual learners disregard these differences and rely on colorblind paradigms that result in deficit portrayals and likely mediate disparities in disability identification rates (Artiles, 2015; Castro et al., 2021).
  > » There has been a historical ambivalence about the value of bilingualism and the need to support bilingual policies and programs (NASEM, 2017). This attitude likely stems from the longstanding ideology of cultural assimilation that has pervaded U.S. history.
  > » "[T]here is no evidence that [students] with disabilities get confused or overwhelmed or have additional difficulties with or negative consequences from learning two (or more) languages" (NASEM, 2017, p. 360).
  > » "Code switching is a normal grammatical and communicatively effective behavior in all [dual language learners/English learners], including those with disabilities" (NASEM, 2017, p. 360).
  > » Contrary to the common recommendation that parents should *not* use their primary language with their child with disabilities, ". . . research findings suggest that speaking the home language facilitates social interaction, and in turn language and social development" (NASEM, 2017, p. 361).

Herrera and her colleagues take these research and historical facts to heart. For this purpose, they start by acknowledging such barriers and offer readers a *cultural toolkit* to understand child development and disabilities. Their critique of canonical frames and practices with students living at the intersections of race, ethnicity, language, and disability raise consequential questions for the future of educational policy, research, and practice. To name a few: How do we re-envision one of the fastest growing communities in our society? What kinds of knowledge do we need to design learning environments and experiences that disrupt the monocultural and monolingual assumptions of educational institutions? What are viable interventions to overcome the overwhelming deficit discourses that pervade in schools and teacher education programs about these students and how can we build teacher capacity to improve their education?

Herrera et al. bet on an asset-oriented standpoint that honors the cultural, social, psychological, emotional, and historical resources that all communities generate and use to face adversity and thrive. Their intervention is grounded in an interdisciplinary vision that braids generations of scholarship centering the role of culture, history, and equity in learning and human development. These include culturally relevant, culturally responsive, and culturally sustaining frameworks. In addition, Herrera and her colleagues trace the genealogies of knowledge that inform their model. They generously recognize how their scholarship benefited from the contributions of individuals and groups of researchers that struggled with the same questions of educational equity. The approach is holistic, accounting not only for cognitive and linguistic dimensions, but also for emotional and relational layers in the education of these learners. In this paradigm, teaching and learning are not restricted to what teachers do and say or what students can/cannot do or how they respond. Herrera et al.'s approach also foregrounds the critical importance of interactional processes and how leveraging "third spaces"—the liminal zone between the official space of classroom instruction and the parallel socioemotional and cognitive labor that students do—affords productive learning opportunities for all students.

The volume's emphasis on biography is distinctive and fruitful for several reasons. First, a foundational principle of learning theory is to build from prior knowledge. A child's biography opens a window into their histories of learning. Moreover, and consistent with the cultural perspective of this volume, a student's biography is regarded as embedded in two temporal axes, namely the cultural histories of his/her communities and his/her everyday experiences across multiple settings. In this sense, a person's biography is nothing less than a hybrid of what is acquired through participation in (racial, social, ethnic, linguistic, gender) communities and what is learned from the idiosyncrasies of their everyday life. This approach, therefore, offers opportunities to understand learning as a multifaceted cultural phenomenon. In other words, the approach guiding the volume interweaves three temporal scales of human development: the unique pathways that individual students forge over time (biography), which in turn are constituted by what is acquired from their cultural communities and what is learned in the unique circumstances of everyday interactions at home, school, peer groups, etc. This is indeed a powerful concept; it challenges educators to transcend the essential other—i.e., a Latina girl is not a mere mirror of her so-called "Latinx culture." It also lifts the richness of hybridity—in this perspective, people are hybrid beings: I represent a unique amalgamation of what my communities pass on to me *and* the peculiarities of my life trajectories. This approach challenges us to avoid stereotypes, but it also compels us to honor the contributions of cultural communities.

I commend Herrera, Rodriguez, Cabral, and Holmes for giving us an impressive cultural toolkit to promote learning and expand educational opportunities for underserved students. Their additive approach reminds us that culture and history matter. Their interdisciplinary framing is a necessary resource to avoid shortcuts that only give us superficial and stereotypical access to cultural models of learning. I am confident that this volume will be an indispensable resource for educators engaged in the cultural work we describe as education.

—Alfredo J. Artiles

REFERENCES

Abramitzky, R., & Boustan, L. (2022). *Streets of gold: America's untold story of immigrant success.* Public Affairs.

Artiles, A. J. (2013). Untangling the racialization of disabilities: An intersectionality critique across disability models. *DuBois Review, 10,* 329–347.

Artiles, A. J. (2015). Beyond responsiveness to identity badges: Future research on culture in disability and implications for RTI. *Educational Review, 67*(1), 1–22.

Artiles, A. J. (2022). Interdisciplinary notes on the dual nature of disability: Disrupting ideology-ontology circuits in racial disparities research. *Literacy Research: Theory, Method, and Practice,* 1–20. https://doi.org/10.1177/23813377221120106

Artiles, A. J., Trent, S. C., & Kuan, L. A. (1997). Learning disabilities research on ethnic minority students: An analysis of 22 years of studies published in selected refereed journals. *Learning Disabilities Research & Practice, 12*, 82–91.

Bonilla-Silva, E., & Baiocchi, G. (2001). Anything but racism: How sociologists limit the significance of racism. *Race & Society, 4*, 117–131. https://doi.org/10.1016/S1090-9524(03)00004-4

Castro, D., Gillanders, C., Prishker, N., & Rodriguez, R. (2021). A sociocultural, integrative, and interdisciplinary perspective on the development and education of young bilingual children with disabilities. In D. Castro & A. J. Artiles (Eds.), *Language, learning and disability in the education of young bilingual children* (pp. 6–26). Multilingual Matters/Center for Applied Linguistics.

Florida, R. (2019). *The rise of the creative class*. Basic Books.

National Academies of Sciences, Engineering, and Medicine (NASEM). (2017). *Promoting the educational success of children and youth learning English: Promising futures*. The National Academies Press. https://doi.org/10.17226/24677

Roberts, S. O., Bareket-Shavit, C., Dollins, F. A., Goldie, P. D. & Mortenson, E. (2020). Racial inequality in psychological research: Trends of the past and recommendations for the future. *Perspectives on Psychological Science, 15*, 1295–1309.

Tefera, A., & Artiles, A. J. (2023). Learning disabilities' unsettling intersections: Betwixt learning, cultural, socioeconomic, and environmental deficiencies. In R. Tierney, F. Rizvi, K. Ercikan, & G. Smith (Eds.), *International Encyclopedia of Education* (4th ed., Vol. 10, pp. 279–287). Elsevier.

Acknowledgments

We acknowledge those individuals who really make the difference, who move beyond words and excuses that limit what is possible in schools. Thus, we first thank the stakeholders, administrators, teachers, and families who advocate daily to challenge old paradigms, even when it doesn't feel comfortable. There is no doubt a foundation, an existing roadmap, that is solid and serves as a guide; however, there is also much to be questioned and re-envisioned to ensure all learners have access to an equitable education. Each of the administrators and teachers highlighted in this book, along with countless others, has contributed to our questioning our own assumptions, reminding us that working within a system is a complex endeavor. Each has a story to tell about how the demographics of their context are ever-changing—unaccompanied minors, new immigrants, 67 languages spoken in one district, and so much more. There has yet to emerge one clear path to assessment, evaluation, placement, and programming for the culturally and linguistically diverse youth of today. Therefore, educators from across the country who have taught us so much remind us that change is slow in coming and that conscious reflection, persistence, and advocacy are critical to moving forward. We thank them for keeping us in check and keeping it real. Without their support, this book never would have been possible.

We thank Teachers College Press for their commitment to our work and vision, allowing us to continue exploring ways that Biography-Driven Instruction can ignite new possibilities for teachers, students, and families. At the press, Jean Ward encouraged us to continue our journey of sharing with others why biography matters. Her words and guidance still speak to the work we do. Emily Spangler provided continued support and editorial expertise along the way. Lynne Frost reviewed this manuscript, posing questions and offering suggestions that helped us clarify our message and ensure consistency across our works. John Bylander brought his keen attention to detail and understanding of the production process, assuring us that a finished product was possible.

Dr. Alfredo Artilles contextualized our work within the longstanding efforts of educators to expose patterns of inequity and to connect research, theory, and practice from multiple disciplines to advance effective pedagogy for emergent bilingual learners. We are grateful for his willingness to share insights gleaned from years of scholarship and dedicated service to the field.

Introduction

As educators, researchers, and advocates who spend a great deal of time in classrooms across the country and all over the world, what has captured our attention is the compartmentalization of human beings with regard to potential. Through categorization based on sociocultural, linguistic, cognitive, and academic labels drawn from policy, program models, curricula, or data, the possibilities for many learners have become circumscribed, especially as experts in the field design "one size fits all" responses to address the multifaceted needs and assets of culturally and linguistically diverse populations.

A birds-eye view of current national trends and statistics provides a glimpse as to how the landscape of this country is changing. During the 2000–2001 academic year, a total of 3,793,764 K–12 English learners (ELs) were enrolled in U.S. public schools, representing 8.1% of all students enrolled (Office of English Language Acquisition, 2020). By the 2019–2020 academic year, the EL population had grown by almost 1.5 million to a total representing 10.4% of total student enrollment (National Center for Education Statistics [NCES], 2021). Most public school teachers (64%) have at least one EL in their classroom (NCES, 2020). Narrowing the view, we find that ELs represent 10% or more of the student population in 12 states; 22 additional states have EL populations that represent between 6% and 10% of students (NCES, 2022). Taken a step further, we find language diversity at the district, school, and classroom level that creates a new landscape in which we are to deliver core instruction that is accessible to all. For example, in one rural Kansas district, more than 45 countries and 20 home languages are represented by the EL population, which comprises 46% of all students.

Determining the learning needs of culturally and linguistically diverse (CLD) students, and especially those who are ELs, requires an awareness of how second-language acquisition processes and emergent bilingual capabilities influence typically expected performance and outcomes. Indicators that educators need increased support to identify and appropriately target such needs are found in the disproportionate representation of ELs in special education, with overrepresentation and underrepresentation varying by context (National Center for Learning Disabilities, 2020). Gutiérrez and colleagues (2017) state that to better meet the needs of all learners, we must be better at exploring the spaces we find ourselves in and teach from a vantage point that visualizes possibilities. They argue that educators need to be prepared to "see ingenuity instead of ineptness and inability, to see resilience instead of deficit" (Gutiérrez et al., 2017, p. 30).

How does one begin to see ingenuity in the learner when the interventions come from a box that assumes the intervention will address "gaps" that the "data" has identified? Where do the assets and history of the learner fit into the conversations we have about CLD students who come to school with a rich linguistic repertoire that often goes untapped, with experiences that never make it into the lesson, and with pathways for processing information that are culturally and linguistically bound?

For many years we have stood on the shoulders of pioneering researchers and educators who have paved the path for what it means to be culturally relevant and responsive in our practices (e.g., Gay, 2000; Ladson-Billings, 1994). More recently, Zaretta Hammond (2015) has detailed how the brain responds to educational contexts that are not culturally responsive. What are the consequences when we do not attend to the potential of the learner? How do we position students to become independent rather than dependent in their educational journey? What considerations are critical when supporting CLD learners who may qualify for special education? Our work with students, teachers, and other educational professionals surrounding such questions has guided us to write this book.

Through each of our own journeys in education, we have come to experience and research the possibilities for all learners in PK–12 classrooms. We are continually advocating for evaluations, assessments, and instruction to be anchored in ecologies where students are provided the space and tools to strengthen their cognitive belief system as learners and develop a *"Sí, se puede"*—that is, a "Yes, I am visible! Yes, I can do it!"—attitude. When all educators take time to consider the diversity in their own contexts, we are better able to see and address the many challenges and caveats that may become limitations for families and students whose biographies may not have been considered when a given policy was enacted, a curriculum was written, or an assessment was developed. It is incumbent on each of us to raise relevant questions and to take into consideration the totality of what the family and learner bring. With a deeper understanding of learners and their realities, we can then bridge from their knowledge to the more standardized ways of doing that we have been conditioned to follow. It is when we are able to achieve this type of dynamic that we educators can profess to be culturally responsive and equitable in our work. Our vision for this textbook is to open up the conversation among educators about the types of considerations that are critical to re-envisioning the future and shedding light on the ever-present question of "Is it language or learning disability?"

Since the passing of the Education for All Handicapped Children Act (1975) and the reauthorization of the Individuals With Disabilities Education Act (IDEA) (1990, 1994, 2004), special education services in schools have a legal basis that defines the procedures and the legalities of assessing and providing instruction for all students at risk of being identified as having a disability. Yet, instructional and pedagogical actions rooted in law have frequently failed to address the casualties of inappropriate placement from the very onset, which often include misidentification and either inappropriate placement in special education services or denial of services. Despite the legal guarantees of a "free and appropriate public education," IDEA works under a limited scope of research surrounding CLD students and families, and its implementation commonly reflects exclusionary interpretation of policies and practices. This myopic view of special education has led to a prescriptive approach in schools that limits the potential and opportunity for CLD learners. The current state of education further exacerbates inequities for students acquiring a second language, because policies and practices frequently impede their ability to maximize and access content, advance in second language acquisition, make academic progress, demonstrate knowledge, and participate in inclusive classrooms. Such conditions inevitably lead to misdiagnosis and inappropriate programming, placement, and instruction.

Critical questions as we seek to ensure equitable educational opportunities for CLD learners are (1) How do students' biopsychosocial histories influence their learning? (2) How do we develop students' strengths through asset-driven programming? (3) How do we create opportunities that maximize learners' potential and capitalize on students' cultural and linguistic assets? and (4) How do we improve the evaluation, assessment, and educational outcomes of CLD students with disabilities? The use of culturally responsive/sustaining pedagogy requires and inspires all participants to delve deeper into understanding and incorporating the biography of the learner in decision-making and instructional processes. An asset-based pedagogy springs from an ecology of empathy and authentic *cariño*—loving care that encourages, supports, and challenges (Valenzuela, 1999)—where any amount of input is fostered and celebrated as students navigate curricular and instructional paths.

The following overview provides a brief summary of the progressive path set forth in this book. Part I (Chapters 1 and 2) contextualizes for the reader the overarching pillars that currently serve to undergird what frames special education contexts and the approaches taken in practice. Part II (Chapters 3, 4, and 5) introduces the reader to biography-driven instruction (BDI) as fundamental to approaching instruction from an assets-based perspective, where decisions are made by documenting the language and knowledge of the learner through a framework that values home and community knowledge and skills. By setting conditions and attending to what the learner produces situationally, educators are able to take the learner from the known to the unknown, thereby always teaching within the learner's zone of proximal development (Vygotsky, 1978). Part III (Chapters 6, 7, and 8) invites readers to dive deeper into practices for serving CLD students with disabilities. We explore how the ability to recognize assets in contexts outside of school can be leveraged during teaching in general education and special education spaces. Part III illuminates intersections of BDI practice and special education policy that lead to more authentic, effective, and lasting outcomes for CLD students and the families in which they live.

Chapter 1 sets the stage for textwide exploration of policy and practice around processes (e.g., instruction, assessment, identification) and service to CLD students with special education needs. The authors reveal ways in which practice has informed theory, and theory in turn shapes practice. An overarching theme explored is the role of public policy and law to support or distract from practices that truly benefit CLD students with disabilities and their families. Chapter 1 begins a journey to shift from filling student-held gaps/deficits and checkbox compliance toward identifying gaps in the educational system through which to reduce the incidence, degree, and impacts of disabling conditions. Recognizing the multidimensionality of students' lives allows us to move two-dimensional activities to three-dimensional results, improving whole systems *for all* while animating the spirit of IDEA for those whom it is designed to protect.

Chapter 2 delves deeply into principles of IDEA, its impact on CLD students, and its potential to assure equitable education for all. Because the principles of IDEA ensure justice and compel action to eliminate inequities, educational systems apply significant weight to compliance with this law. In this chapter, the authors present major principles of IDEA as described by statute, but also prevalent caveats to interpretation and considerations for ethical adherence. Areas addressed in detail include (1) Child Find/zero reject, (2) nondiscriminatory evaluation, (3) individualized education programs (IEPs), (4) related services, (5) least restrictive environment (LRE), (6) parent participation, and (7) procedural safeguards, as they relate to the needs and rights of CLD students and their families.

Integral to any consideration of referral is the degree to which prereferral and intervention practices reflect data informed by the life of the student, contextualized by limitations of the probes/impressions underlying the impetus to refer.

Chapter 3 explores issues based on IDEA with respect to the guidance provided on the rights of the learner and the responsibility of schools and educators. The process for answering the question of appropriate programming often begins with the goal that a CLD learner be placed in the setting that is the most "accommodating" to provide them with the necessary support systems that will increase their social and academic success. This chapter illustrates how teachers can navigate instructional processes, based on where the learner is on the continuum of prereferral for testing, referral, and monitoring to ensure that all CLD learners experience access, engagement, and hope. We explore what it means to understand the learner through a prism of possibilities by considering how four dimensions of the student biography (sociocultural, linguistic, cognitive, and academic) intersect with the learner's biopsychosocial history to influence the learner's engagement, motivation, and cognitive belief system.

Chapter 4 expands on the notion of an ecology of respect and authentic *cariño* through a focus on the role that joint productive activity plays in inclusive classroom practices. Educators are guided to harvest and document what students know, and then utilize the insights to create a community where knowledge is socially and academically constructed through collaboration-focused interaction. This chapter addresses how a tool in the hand supports learners to interact in ways that foster development along each dimension of their biography (sociocultural, linguistic, cognitive, and academic) as they progress toward attainment of the standards-driven learning goals. The authors illustrate how biography-driven strategies can be used to scaffold and enrich learning opportunities for *all* students. This perspective is provided to help teachers explore the language, knowledge, and skills of CLD learners, including those with disabilities.

Chapter 5 highlights the importance of maximizing classroom talk to build an inclusive classroom community. Through strategies rooted in the principles of BDI, this chapter illustrates how instructional conversations can be orchestrated to foster trust, maximize the diversity of learners present, and nurture a culturally and linguistically responsive ecology. The authors provide excerpts of classroom talk to illustrate how instructional conversations center the learner, involve a reciprocal ebb and flow of communication, and reflect equitable patterns of interaction. Teachers are encouraged to situationally attend to what learners do and say in order to weave their words and ideas into the lesson, advance their conceptual understanding, and support their language and literacy development. We discuss how to engage students in dialogic exchanges that honor and maximize the unique human potential of each learner, thereby fostering teaching and learning in the "third space" (Gutiérrez et al., 2003).

Chapter 6 provides examples of how general education and special education teachers can address IEP goals for oral language development through BDI. The chapter seeks to bridge the languages of inclusive BDI and special education to create comprehensible interpretations and responses to the most common IEP goals for oral communication. Included among these are activities to: (1) improve speech sounds, (2) increase expressive language (quantity, use, structure), (3) expand content understandings/use (vocabulary, semantics), (4) demonstrate comprehension, (5) ask questions for a purpose, (6) answer questions to affirm or explain, (7) retell a story or event, (8) summarize a story or text, and (9) increase speech fluency. The authors detail specific examples of goal behaviors and straightforward ways to support each area of communication development.

Chapter 7 addresses how the restrictiveness of traditional curricula and settings for students with "low-incidence" disabilities (e.g., hearing, vision, cognitive, and/or intersecting) can be lessened through incorporation of BDI. The authors draw upon medical and social models of disability to demonstrate the impact of "ableist" culture on educator lenses regarding students with low-incidence disabilities, especially those whose cultural ideals and languages differ from those of majority groups. The authors provide a list of accommodations that includes specific practices to enable equitable participation within each community of learners. We also include discussion of how the three overarching modes of access proposed by universal design for learning (UDL) intersect with BDI.

Chapter 8 brings the reader full circle by sharing the voices of two additional researchers/special education practitioners who pose difficult questions framed by theory, research, and practice. Although the questions have no absolute answers, they allow educators to grapple with the most appropriate paths to take, with the knowledge and tools they have, to move forward toward equity, respect, and possibility. The chapter offers a description of one district's efforts to transform instructional practices, family involvement, and student achievement. It also positions the reader to reflect on the complexities that must be addressed in policy and practice to meet the needs of CLD learners, including those being considered for referral, in the referral process, or receiving special education services, in culturally and linguistically responsive ways. As researchers and educators, our hope is that this chapter creates a space for the work that still needs to be done by highlighting the responsibility each of us has to make it happen.

Our work is presented here for educators to join us in charting new paths that acknowledge where and how we can do better. Together, using the research that is available to push back on "one size fits all" agendas, we can begin to see and involve families as true partners in mapping a destination for their children that acknowledges the rich history and language present in their homes and communities. Baca and Cervantes opened the door, Klingner furthered the conversation, and Artiles challenged us to do better. We have the roadmaps. The question becomes, *Will we as educators embark on the journey?*

Part I

HISTORICALLY CENTERING THE STUDENT THROUGH IDEA

Searching for Coal in a Gold Mine
Overlooking the Multifaceted Assets of the Learner

The wrongs done to . . . language minority students in special education are exceptionally severe: misidentification, misplacement, misuse of tests, and poor academic performance within special education. (Ruiz, 1989, p. 139)

Decades have passed since Ruiz (1989) documented the inequitable educational practices experienced by many emergent bilingual students, yet the research and conversation on special education for culturally and linguistically diverse (CLD) learners continue to circle back to distinguishing language difference from disability. Questions such as the following have merit in moving the conversation forward:

- In what ways do general education teachers describe their teaching and factors they consider when making decisions related to prereferral and referral processes for CLD learners?
- What are the range and types of concerns noted by classroom teachers when CLD students are referred for special education evaluation?
- What types of interventions have been implemented by the time CLD learners are referred for special education evaluation?
- Are special education services being considered even for CLD students who are *not* found to be innately disabled?
- In what ways, if any, do child study team members' use of data and decision-making for CLD students reflect entrenched perspectives on systems and practices?
- Do referring teachers report feeling adequately prepared by their preservice and/or inservice training to teach CLD students?

IN SEARCH OF ANSWERS

Conversations on the theory-to-praxis gap have long persisted in faculty and teacher lounges, with both groups continually lamenting the question of how out of touch one group is with the other. However, if we follow the path between questions posed about practice by educators in the field, and the research of the most prominent faculty in the field, we will find that both raise similar questions and make recommendations that inevitably lead us down the same path toward the need for educators to understand and distinguish disability from linguistic and cultural difference.

From Practice to Theory

Cabral (2008), after years of work within her district, sought to address the pressing questions that were front and center in daily work. For decades, the disproportionally large number of CLD students being referred for, and placed in, special education persisted. Regardless of trainings, practices reported during this study revealed assumptions in evaluation that threatened validity of assessments used in the referral and placement of CLD students. The teachers lacked preparation to distinguish between difference due to the diversity of the learner being referred and difference resulting from a potentially present disability. What was most problematic was that once students were referred, they were highly likely to be placed in special education without further thought. Referral was based on the failure of CLD students to perform as expected on interventions that had not accommodated for the sociocultural, linguistic, or cognitive dimensions of the learner. Therefore, results of interventions and accommodations served to reinforce teacher perceptions of prereferral as a confirmatory process rather than a process of determining how student learning challenges could be resolved.

These phenomena were compounded by the teachers' expressed deference for psychological test data and preference for special education placement. Additionally, teachers' opinions about CLD student language proficiencies, based on observation, often led to instruction and intervention processes that increased the number of inappropriate referrals for special education. Cabral's journey pushed her to pursue research to determine the validity of teacher impressions as well as methods by which teachers could better identify and respond to CLD students' language assets and needs. Cabral's (2008) study is but one example of how dilemmas of practice provide the impetus for research that seeks to further our understanding of the issues involved and shed light on possible factors that might lead to enhanced pedagogical effectiveness and educational equity.

Bridging Theory into Practice

Research (e.g., Thomas & Collier, 1997, 2002) has long documented the phenomenon of CLD learners being inappropriately placed in learning settings that fail to attend to the multiple dimensions of their identities and lived experiences, leading to reduced opportunities to learn. Thomas and Collier identified the instructional models utilized in U.S. classrooms as pivotal factors contributing to the miseducation of emergent bilingual learners. Students are prevented from full access to the grade-level curriculum when instruction fails to attend to their unique sociocultural, linguistic, cognitive, and academic assets and needs. What results are achievement discrepancies that educators frequently interpret at face value rather than exploring the classroom conditions, scaffolds, and modifications that can allow learners to actualize their true potential. Such discrepancies are perceived as achievement gaps rather than opportunity gaps. In fact, achievement gaps noted in

the grade-level classroom are a leading reason that teachers refer CLD learners for special education (Hosp & Reschly, 2004).

The overwhelming tendency is for referred CLD students to be identified as having a disability regardless of whether they truly do have an innate learning difficulty, and this pattern leads to learners being placed in more restrictive learning settings than is appropriate (Artiles et al., 2005; De Valenzuela et al., 2006). Such settings can be detrimental for all CLD learners, because they typically fail to result in improved academic gains compared to general education settings, even for those students who are eligible and demonstrate need for special education (Maldonado, 1994; Wilkerson & Ortiz, 1986). Why is this? Simply put, emergent bilingual learners need opportunities to acquire English language through authentic interactions with their peers while simultaneously expanding their conceptual knowledge and skills through an academically rigorous and scaffolded curriculum. Teachers' experiences with CLD learners, their knowledge of second language acquisition theory, and their understanding of effective practice—including ways to assess, interpret, and respond to what CLD students produce—directly influence the academic success of diverse learners.

Policy Meets Practice

Reports to Congress on the implementation of the Individuals With Disabilities Education Act (IDEA) (e.g., U.S. Department of Education, 2002) have provided data that continually reveal CLD students to be overrepresented in educational programs for the disabled and underrepresented in those designed for the most capable students. Over the years, reasons cited for these types of outcomes include:

- Instructional models that have not provided the cultural and linguistic support for CLD learners to access the grade-level curriculum (Thomas & Collier, 1997, 2002)
- Lack of teachers prepared to meet the multidimensional (sociocultural, linguistic, cognitive, and academic) needs of a very diverse population (Banerjee & Luckner, 2014; Kolano et al., 2014; Madler et al., 2022; Symeou & Karagiorgi, 2018; Walton et al., 2005)

- Overreliance on standardized assessments for the determination of disability (Baca & Cervantes, 2004; Frey, 2019; Maki & Adams, 2020)
- Student response to interventions that (1) do not involve the parents (Goldman & Burke, 2017); (2) do not address linguistic or cultural barriers to learning (Ford, 2012); (3) fail to align instruction with student learning abilities (Herrera, Cabral, & Murry, 2020); and/or (4) do not reflect a process of collaboration, instructional modification, results evaluation, and revision over time (Reyes, 2022)

The persistence of such patterns of over/underrepresentation of CLD students indicates a disconnect between policy intentions and student outcomes. Charting the next steps forward will require that we find new ways to infuse the spirit of the laws and policies into our systems and processes. As educators, we also must anchor our pedagogical efforts solidly in the theory and research on effective instructional practices for learners who bring nondominant cultures and languages. For teachers and other educational professionals, "building on the best" from research, theory, policy, and practice will mean collaborating to leverage our collective knowledge, ingenuity, skills, and creativity toward the shared goal of altering the learning trajectory for CLD learners, including those being considered for or receiving services in special education programs.

BEYOND A DEFICIT PERSPECTIVE: EXPLORING GAPS IN SYSTEMS

Theory, practice, and policy have clearly documented the **deficit perspective** often found within decision-making processes during prereferral, referral, placement, and ultimately the services provided to CLD students. The prevalence of deficit orientations has not changed over the last 50 years, since Dr. Leonard Baca, considered by many to be the grandfather of bilingual special education, and the many doctoral students who followed started researching, writing, and providing professional development services to districts on these issues. Baca raised the initial questions surrounding the overrepresentation of emergent bilinguals being referred to special education. He was relentless in asking questions related to the reliability and validity of standardized instruments utilized in the decision-making process. He recognized the importance of providing instruction that was grounded in the cultures and communities of the learner, as well as the importance of the learner and teacher producing together.

In a seminal work, Baca and Amato (1989) shared a core set of principles considered central to addressing the needs of families and students. Key was the teachers' willingness to engage with parents and learners from a culturally responsive and sustaining stance by seeking to understand the communities, homes, languages, and cultures of the students they were teaching. The teachers' knowledge of effective programming, instructional methods, and nonbiased assessment was also of critical importance. From this work we have gleaned the fundamentals that are central to meeting the needs of CLD students, and these have not changed over multiple decades of research and practice in describing what "should" and "could" be accomplished in classroom practice.

Others whom we (the authors of this text) consider heroes include the late Dr. Janette Klingner, whose research surfaced key concepts around practices that we continue to address. Klingner's expertise and studies were inspired by her own experiences as a teacher of bilingual special education. That lens informed and gave life to specializations in the *applications* of educational theories around reading, response to intervention (RTI) for English learners, and the impact of systems to drive or diminish outcomes for CLD students.

Specifically, the works of Klingner and colleagues (e.g., Harry & Klingner, 2014; Klingner et al., 2005, 2008; Klingner & Vaughn, 2002) invited us to explore factors contributing to the disproportionate representation of CLD students in special education. Her work shed light on disconnects in instruction and measurement that arise from overgeneralization of the "Big Five" (phonemic awareness, phonics, fluency, vocabulary, and comprehension) (National Reading Panel et al., 2000) to *universally* meet every learner's needs. She inspired us to ask how relinquishing default remedies could allow us to leverage the linguistic and experiential assets of CLD students. Klingner's reminders that intervention is intended to be an evolving and self-strengthening process of data collection, collaboration, instructional modification, evaluation, and intervention, *repeated over time*, begs our continued attention to the realities of this process. Indeed, the circular nature of systems, models, and opportunity to learn factors significantly into our abilities to respond to disabled students and/or the disabling conditions created for students.

Dr. Alfredo Artiles is arguably the premier researcher today on topics related to CLD students and special education. His decades of contributions continue to influence studies and conversations around previously simplified questions. Early on, Artiles led us beyond asking whether a "student's problem" was related to language or disability. He invited us into spaces that examined myriad variables and the uncomfortable dissonance between theories that "explain" overrepresentation—except when they don't. For example, if poverty is a factor in disability determination, why does the impact appear to vary by race? The work of Artiles (e.g., Artiles, 2022; Artiles & Ortiz, 2002; Artiles et al., 2005) prompts special educators and evaluators to see other patterns and explore new questions, such as:

- Why does it seem that students in English-only programs who may have experienced language loss (from disuse) are so often referred for special education?
- How is it that such students are much more likely to be identified with cognitive impairments *at the secondary level* than students whose similar exceptionality is apparent much earlier in life?
- What are the placement outcomes for students identified as needing special education?
- Why do levels of restrictiveness and segregation appear to differ by factors outside the qualifying criteria?

Artiles's research and collaborations have changed every dynamic of discussion around *why* we place students in special education and *what happens* as a result. He challenges us to consider deeply embedded issues of racial disparities in education and whether/how school responses to matters of compliance alter the nature and equity of practice.

THE FOUNDATION OF AN ASSET-DRIVEN AGENDA

Changing the direction of outcomes for CLD students, including exceptional learners with innate disabilities and gifts, requires a new outlook on teaching and learning informed by a deeper understanding and responsiveness to members of our classroom communities. Foundational research and scholarship ground the philosophy, methodology, instructional strategies, and perspectives of special education processes and practices highlighted throughout this book. This chapter highlights some of the most fundamental solutions to effectively serving learners who bring diverse cultural and linguistic assets and experiences.

Culturally Relevant/Responsive/Sustaining Teaching

Our work continues the legacy of equity pedagogies that find their roots in the ideas of innovators and leaders such as Dr. Gloria Ladson-Billings. Through *culturally relevant pedagogy*, Ladson-Billings (1994) charged educators to step outside uniform (monocultural) approaches curriculum and instruction to instead use the histories, knowledge, and skills of CLD students as a springboard to success in school. Ladson-Billings reminded educators that not all learning and growth can be captured on standardized assessments. She challenged us to expand our perspectives on culture beyond the more visible/tangible (but also superficial) elements of culture (e.g., customs, artifacts, foods) to explore the beliefs, values, and ways of knowing that undergird learners' interpretations and connections to the curriculum. She illustrated how confronting deficit perspectives in education requires us to first understand our own positionality. Knowing who we are and how we fit in the world, including implications for access and power, is a necessary step toward understanding how best to support and advocate for CLD learners inside and outside the school walls.

We further anchor our own practices in the research and scholarship of Dr. Geneva Gay. Gay pioneered *culturally responsive teaching*, which she characterized in her seminal work as validating, comprehensive, multidimensional, empowering, transformative, and emancipatory (Gay, 2000). Her goal was to ensure that learners' lived experiences in their homes and communities, and the wealth of knowledge and assets that resulted, were maximized with the classroom context. Gay reminded us that educating the whole child includes attending to the intellectual, social, emotional, and political aspects of learning. Education is not about creating compliant students; rather, it is about supporting each learner to actively engage in the challenge and the wonder of constructing knowledge by sharing, reflecting, thinking critically, and feeling. Gay spotlighted the importance of teachers who affirm every CLD learner's value, capabilities, and academic potential. Learning spaces can be psychologically and academically liberating when we allow learners to use their multidimensional assets, histories, and ways of knowing to explore the curriculum, become engaged producers of knowledge, and take ownership of their role in solving problems and creating a better world.

We additionally have been informed by the work of Dr. Django Paris (e.g., Paris, 2012; Alim & Paris, 2017). In his groundbreaking work, Paris (2012) challenged educators to consider the extent to which we have made the ideals of culturally relevant pedagogy and culturally responsive teaching a reality for CLD learners in today's schools and classrooms. While acknowledging and affirming the intent of prior equity- and asset-focused approaches, Paris reminded us of the need to do more than just utilize learners' assets as a means to support their "success" in school as typically conceived. The current standards, benchmarks, and curricula need not dictate a singular view of what it means to succeed in school (and beyond). Rather, through his envisioning of *culturally sustaining pedagogies* (Paris, 2012), he asks us to "perpetuate and foster—to sustain—linguistic, literate, and cultural pluralism as part of the democratic project of schooling" (2012, p. 93). Creating equitable spaces for students from every background to leverage their identities (e.g., heritage and community practices, languages, family literacy practices) and contribute as equal members benefits *all* learners.

It is from this foundation that **biography-driven instruction (BDI)** (Herrera, 2010, 2016, 2022) has evolved. At its core, the BDI framework centralizes the sociocultural, linguistic, cognitive, and academic dimensions of the learner's biography, which is situated within the learners' biopsychosocial history. These constructs are explored throughout the subsequent chapters of this book to illustrate how educators can develop a more thorough, multifaceted understanding of CLD learners. With a greater awareness of the assets that students bring as well as the challenges and transitions they may encounter, educators can engage in more culturally and linguistically responsive ways, developing and implementing increasingly effective lessons, instructional scaffolds, interventions, and individualized programming. The shift toward discovering and utilizing students' words, knowledge systems, literacies, skills, and experiences has the power to illuminate new possibilities for actualizing the potential of each learner.

Creating a Hybrid Space for Learning

In BDI, the goal is to create learning spaces that invite learners in to participate *with us* on a shared learning journey. As educators, we bring specialized knowledge of the content, the curriculum, special education programming and processes, and the language of the school. We also bring our own biographies, including experiences, values, and ways of viewing the world that have developed through our childhood, adolescence, and adult life (e.g., college, teacher preparation, employment, relationships, parenting). Students likewise bring expertise about their own lived realities. Yet, often, learners are asked to set aside what they bring and instead view learning and the content through the eyes of the teacher or the textbook.

Dr. Kris Gutiérrez and her colleagues (e.g., Gutiérrez et al., 2003) use the concept of the **third space** to describe the teaching and learning dynamics that result when we create spaces where teachers and students come together to ask questions, exchange ideas, share connections, grapple with incongruities, and think critically and creatively about how the content relates to the classroom community, society, and larger world. In the third space, we build on individual and cumulative assets, drawing from both teacher discourse (the official space of the classroom) and student discourse (the unofficial space of learners' lives). Teachers provide opportunities for student talk to take center stage, utilizing different forms of participation and allowing for fluid shifts in power, such that educators and students are variously enacting the roles of teacher and learner.

In the third space, *all* members of the classroom community are encouraged and supported to draw upon their full repertoire of resources. BDI provides strategies and tools to structure the flow of learning and scaffold students' participation and engagement from their individual points of entry. By first activating what learners know, teachers and students are positioned to readily make connections between the known (background knowledge) and the unknown (new concepts and language). Opportunities to interact with the teacher(s) and peers then allow everyone to benefit from a plurality of perspectives.

Voices From the Field

I feel like kids realize that, kids know who has special needs. They know these kids, you know. So, when you use something like this [the U-C-ME BDI strategy], kids don't really seem to care. You know, they don't really seem to care who's the emergent [bilingual], who's special ed, they don't really care about that. It's more like, "Ok, what do you know about this?" . . . it's becoming more like a community and not labeling the kids. . . .

—Emily Green, Elementary ESOL
(English for speakers of other languages) Teacher

Humanistic Relationships of Love, Belonging, and Hope

Dr. Angela Valenzuela reminds us that in education, everything boils down to the care that we have for one another as fellow human beings. Valenzuela's (1999) concept of **authentic *cariño*** reminds educators that truly caring about learners includes love *and beyond*. It means sharing in their joys and struggles and working together to ensure everyone

succeeds. When we create conditions for authentic *cariño* to flourish, we communicate to each member of the classroom community that they belong. We also pave the way for learners to experience success with social, academic, and language development that leads to hope for educational performance today and a bright future in the years to come.

For authentic *cariño* to become a reality, we must broaden the circle to include families and communities in how we come to understand learners and their assets, needs, and realities. An exchange of ideas and a willingness to collaborate across differences depends, however, on relational trust (Bryk & Schneider, 2002). As Herrera, Porter, and Barko-Alva (2020) note, "fostering authentic *cariño* is reliant on our feeling deeply for one another, humbly unlearning divisive ways of thinking and doing, and envisioning a tomorrow that reflects the voices of all community members" (p. 78). Parents/caregivers, families, educators, and other community members all bring years of accumulated experiences with schooling, with the balance of good versus bad differing along innumerable axes of experience. For all involved, developing relational trust entails a willingness to truly hear others' perspectives. We as educators further have a professional and ethical responsibility to critically reflect on the *why* and *how* of processes and practices currently utilized. When we are able to step outside our typical ways of being, seeing, knowing, and doing, we reap the benefits of a more nuanced, pluralistic, and cross-culturally competent perspective (Jordan et al., 2017; Porter, 2018; Pratt-Johnson, 2006). Chief among such outcomes are the enhanced well-being and success of all CLD learners, irrespective of (dis)ability.

CONCLUSION

Without a doubt, for many of us educators the struggles, challenges, and questions surrounding CLD learners and special education have changed very little during the course of our professional lives. These questions hang heavy across districts that serve high numbers of CLD students and struggle with preparing, teaching, finding appropriate assessment tools, and attending to the moral imperative to do the right thing by centering families in the decision-making process surrounding programming and services that will best meet the needs of their children.

In the Voices From the Field textbox, the words of Ms. Green attest to the potential of the U-C-ME biography-driven strategy (see Chapter 5 and Appendix A for description of this strategy) to create the classroom conditions that enable learners to see peers beyond their limitations and to be more in tune with their potential. These are the types of conditions we as researchers and educators seek to create during Tier 1 instruction, Tier 2 interventions, and Tier 3 support. Such conditions are predicated on the teacher seeing learners for their potential by harvesting what they know in order to scaffold their learning toward increasingly complex levels of thought and language use. The researchers and practitioners highlighted in this chapter have already cracked the code for attending to what works. Chapter 2 further opens the door to digging deeper into IDEA and RTI by naming the challenges faced in schools, the caveats that often hinder our ability to step into new ways of doing, and the considerations we as professionals must make in order to do the right thing for CLD students when determining the best instructional practices for each individual learner.

CHAPTER 1 QUESTIONS FOR REFLECTION AND DISCUSSION

As educators, the first step toward undoing, rethinking, and reimagining is to reflect upon the three C's—challenges, caveats, and considerations—that impact our practices. As professionals in a field that has so many competing agendas, it is critical to reflect upon about our views and perspectives and the role we play in making a difference in the lives of students and families. Reflect on this chapter and independently or collectively with a team, take a position on how you would respond to the following questions.

Challenges

1. How does research inform your practice?
2. How do you explore both sides of an issue and take a position, taking theory into practice based on the population you serve?

Caveats

1. What influence does the sociopolitical context of your state, district, and school have on your position?
2. How do you adjust to align practices with the research when opportunities are driven by longstanding policies and procedures?

Considerations

1. In what ways is it possible to align with research and find the possibilities within longstanding ways of doing?
2. How will you use the information from this chapter to question and guide your learning as you continue reading and learning from the chapters that follow?

CHAPTER 2

Setting the Stage for Cognitive and Socioemotional Resilience

Reflecting on the Intersection of Policy and Systems

You know I had a special education class when I was an undergraduate. It was much like my multicultural class, however, with kids you refer . . . well . . . there is the law to consider. I don't remember talking about kids who don't speak English, but my school has a strict policy not to even look at them because of all this talk about there being too many of them in special education and how will we know if it's a language difference or a disability. We've had some workshops, but I can't even keep up with my planning and teaching. It's just too much sometimes.

—Middle School Teacher, Anonymous

The paths to untangling the complexities of meeting the sociocultural, linguistic, cognitive, and academic challenges faced by culturally and linguistically diverse (CLD) learners are as dynamic and unique as a prism that responds to the angle of the light that shines upon it. As was detailed in Chapter 1, much has been written about these challenges, as well as federal, state, and local responses to the needs of CLD populations. This chapter attempts to address the challenges, caveats, and considerations for educators in providing appropriate evaluation, placement, and services that create equitable learning spaces for CLD learners.

IDEA: WITH THE BEST OF INTENTIONS . . . HAVE WE ARRIVED?

At the federal level we are provided with clear definitions for ensuring that children receive the services they need to be successful in school. Offices such as the U.S. Department of Education (USDE) Office of Special Education Programs (OSEP) exist to review and monitor state efforts in meeting the requirements of the **Individuals With Disabilities Education Act (IDEA)**. IDEA (2004) identifies core principles upon which the law was based. These principles, predicated on the

right of every qualified person to receive a **free and appropriate public education (FAPE)**, include the following: (1) Child Find/zero reject, (2) nondiscriminatory evaluation, (3) individualized education program (IEP), (4) related services, (5) least restrictive environment (LRE), (6) parent participation, and (7) procedural safeguards. Following is a brief overview of the major principles of IDEA, along with challenges, caveats, and considerations for each.

Child Find

The principle of **Child Find** requires each school district to identify students who might need special education services. Federal law requires every state to operate a Child Find process that includes all children from birth to age 21. Although sponsored by public schools, such children may be "found" in private schools, home schools, homeless situations, foster care, institutions, and so forth. The intent of Child Find is to ensure access to publicly funded services for all students with need who reside in each of the 50 states and U.S. territories.

Challenges—Child Find processes may be impacted by the mindsets and training of personnel involved in screenings and/or the appropriateness

14

of tools used to gauge aspects of linguistic and cognitive development. Indicators of gross and fine motor skills are often less affected by subjective interpretation or selection of assessment tools; however, these areas can also depend on individual students' opportunities to practice culture-laden skills, especially as they relate to self-care and family dispositions around independence versus interdependence. Other points of disconnect between the intention and the outcomes of Child Find may result from (1) misperceptions that delays noted may be typical of, or overly attributed to, the child's bilingualism or (2) lack of evaluators' experience with home language(s) other than English.

Caveats—The success of Child Find to locate *all* students with need hinges on community outreach, families' abilities to attend scheduled screenings, and the socio/linguistic/professional assets of personnel who conduct the screening.

Considerations—Questions to foster self-assessment surrounding this principle of IDEA include the following:

- What agencies and media are involved in "getting the word out" about Child Find to all communities represented in our area?
- Do our outreach materials and activities assume literacy on the part of families?
- What skills and dispositions do we look for in staffing Child Find intake and screenings?
- Do we have an established cadre of interpreters with training on the processes and rationales for screening?
- How can we support families in need of transportation to attend screenings?

Nondiscriminatory Evaluation

The principle of **nondiscriminatory evaluation** mandates that measures used to determine eligibility and need in any area of special education be culturally and linguistically nondiscriminatory. Toward this end, the evaluation should be conducted in the language of the student (see Figure 8.1 for additional details) and administered by trained and knowledgeable personnel. Evaluators must *not* rely on any single measure but must include a variety

of tools and strategies to gather functional, developmental, and academic information. Assessment tools and techniques must be deemed technically sound and appropriate for use with the individual student.

Challenges—Many challenges exist in this area. Foremost are those encountered any time evaluation mindsets and processes value scores over information about the conditions under which a student *does* succeed. Compounding threats to validity (e.g., normative base of the test), single measures and point-in-time assessments are subject to numerous variables related to the person(s) involved, situational factors, and appropriateness of the test/task to measure the targeted knowledge or skill. Other risks to nondiscriminatory assessment accompany assumptions that an evaluator can readily determine the child's (presumably one) "language of use." Dichotomous (either/or) thinking around language denies the realities of students and families who dynamically draw upon assets of two or more languages to communicate within and about their worlds.

Caveats—Given the number of languages present across the country, there exist limitations during all phases of the special education (SPED) process. From the first "universal" screeners and onward, assumptions inherent to tests begin to stratify students in ways that can set opinions and expectations uncomfortably low. These perceptions may lead to placements in interventions or groups that focus more on filling a perceived or measured "gap" than inviting students to dive deeper into a more rigorous learning space. Assessment formats that assume "reliability" of indicators based on English speakers, or conflate skill sets (e.g., written versus oral or pictured answers), blind us to what students know and can do. It does not work, however, to merely provide multiple means of expression *during assessment*. Special educators know that accommodations for assessment must reflect conditions present *during instruction*.

Considerations—Teachers' knowledge and agency are critical to convey *and advocate for* the conditions and practices necessary to ensure equity and access to high-quality instruction. Part of this conversation may entail questioning the limitations of assessment:

- Are any of the presumed skill sets (e.g., English proficiency, writing skills) unrelated to the acquisition of the content understandings we aim to probe?
- Does the assessment format hinder students' demonstration and validation of learning?
- Does discussion around assessment results create climates and practices aligned more with attainment of *scores* than *processes* of inquiry, reflection, and discourse?

Individualized Education Programs

The **individualized education program (IEP)** is a plan or program developed to ensure that a child with an identified disability (at the elementary or secondary level) receives specialized instruction and related services. Every IEP (or differently titled document with the same purpose) should include statements addressing/including the student's (1) **present level of academic achievement and functional performance (PLAAFP)**, (2) parent input, (3) annual educational goals, (4) accommodations and modifications, (5) free and appropriate public education (FAPE), and (6) transition plan (see also Figure 8.1).

Challenges—In relation to this IDEA principle, challenges surround the question, How well does the IEP describe *this* individual child? Educators should do the following:

- Ensure that the strengths and weaknesses noted in PLAAFPs include those demonstrated through the home language and student capacities evident outside of school.
- Elicit and document details related to parental views.
- Take into account parent/caregiver insights when developing accommodations and/or goals.
- Address the role of home language in special considerations for IEP implementation.
- Ensure stated goals address distinctions between skills that are undeveloped and

those not evident (yet) in the language or literacy of school.

- Include evidence of response to probes *beyond* universal screeners or standardized tests. For example, a student who does not readily show skills (e.g., sound blending, decoding, repetition for memory) on the marketed test items may nevertheless perform well when the words are drawn from word banks of their own oral use.
- Include descriptions of the student's response to dynamic assessments.

Caveats—Educators who develop plans for IEPs are often constrained to formats or platforms that, ironically, can inhibit *individualization* for CLD students. Disconnects occur when a student is not marked as "Limited English Proficient" (because they don't fit that designation), yet the student is bilingual and unable to access their entire language system when faced with standardized IQ or language assessments in English that were normed on English-only speakers. Another point of disconnect can be the yes/no answer required to the critical statement defining whether the student's difficulty is primarily related to English language proficiency. What if unaccommodated instruction is a factor, in addition to disability?

Considerations—As we consider the IEP developed for a particular learner, we must ask ourselves this question:

- How well does *this* IEP describe *this* individual child, including unique language assets, accommodations for language supports, and where feasible, use of the native language?

Related Services

Related services include transportation and other supportive services as are required to assist a child with a disability to benefit from special education. Related services include speech-language pathology and audiology services, interpreting services, psychological services, physical and occupational therapy, counseling services, orientation and mobility services, school-based health services, and social work services.

Challenges—Challenges regarding related services often involve communications between family members and professionals. Related service providers may need to think outside of the box for ideas on the usefulness and practice of skills in the home setting. Parents will be the best informants once we stop assuming everyone does things in the same way. A great example is the parent who, after being told by the occupational therapist to purchase Play Doh for hand strength, paused to ask, "Why can't she just help me roll and shape the tortillas?"

Caveats—Related service providers (and others) are sometimes guided by checklists that prescribe the way skills are commonly demonstrated. The student who does not "button their own jacket" may adeptly create knots or bait complicated traps. Another may crochet but present with an awkward pencil grasp.

Considerations—Considerations related to this principle involve our thinking beyond our own socialized lens and typical ways of doing. When working with CLD learners, related service providers and teachers are encouraged to wonder

- What might the assessed skills look like in differing contexts?
- How can we reframe the questions we ask?

Least Restrictive Environment

Access to a free and appropriate public education includes the right of students with disabilities to receive the services and supports necessary to access education in the least restrictive environment possible. In educational contexts, **least restrictive environment (LRE)** refers to the environment (e.g., class, peers, instructional modes) wherein the student can maximally access the general education curriculum. For many learners, LRE is found in the general education classroom with specified accommodations or supports. Consideration of LRE must look beyond academic structures and products. For example, a student with a disability in writing (putting ideas and knowledge to paper) may not show mastery of social studies or science content on written tests as well as they otherwise would during discussion, art (e.g., mural), or procedural/

event demonstration. This student should not be disenfranchised from learning opportunities on the basis of their ability to perform types of assessment that conflate content knowledge with other areas, including language. Furthermore, critical socialization and language development occur in contexts with general education peers. As one teacher noted, "I keep reminding myself. How does Giovanni function at home? Is he restricted to a special room in the house, or does he function with others, as able, in the context of simply being 'home'? Why would we expect and provide less at school?"

Challenges—Challenges to LRE take many forms. One is the delay of support and identification for students with true need. Students with unrecognized assets or those placed in restrictive environments due to test scores or performance resulting from combined disenfranchisement (language, culture, and disability) are also effectively denied FAPE. Incalculable harm can occur when students acquiring English are placed in settings with limited access to nondisabled English-speaking peers. Ironically, such denial of FAPE, *resulting from denial of FAPE*, can perpetuate perceptions that these students were "that low" all along.

Caveats—Students hindered from full access to public education may fall victim to reinforcing cycles of poor educational expectations, experiences, and outcomes.

Considerations—What does LRE look like for each student, in each setting and *social, linguistic*, and *cognitive* space? LRE is an individually and contextually situated consideration. Questions to consider include these:

- Do our processes for identifying students' assets and needs respect each learner as an individual fully entitled to education at its best—at *our* best?
- Do our placements embody this ideal?

Parent Participation

Parent participation is necessary to ensure that the opinions, experiences, and perceptions of the parent are sought and considered throughout every stage of referral, assessment, placement, and IEP development. The active word is participation. Information provided by parents is necessary to confirm or disconfirm impressions created in the hypercontextualized setting of school. Parental insights are among the most powerful to inform an individual student's connections to learning or application of skills. How many students who "hate math" nevertheless enjoy sports statistics or leveraging point systems in video games?

Challenges—There can be several challenges to ensuring parents' opportunities to participate in discussions and processes around the student. Despite the proliferation of cell phones, many parents change their devices, carriers, and phone numbers more frequently than are updated at the school. Establishing positive relationships early and maintaining contact (including multiple avenues of contact) are among the highest leverage actions teachers can take to support students. Yet, even when communications are successful, there is a tendency among educators to discount parents' perspectives and information if they differ from how the child is perceived at school (see Chapter 8 for additional discussion related to involving parents and caregivers).

Caveats—Minimizing or disregarding the outcomes of parent participation leads to uninformed interventions and effectively derails appropriate consideration of disability. IDEA requires parental input for a reason. Not only is it simply good practice to involve parents throughout any process related to their child, but parents/guardians can also provide a wealth of insight to, and collaboration around, the needs of the learner.

Considerations—When parents describe the student in ways that differ from school, educators are encouraged to be curious and affirming. Ask questions to gain additional information and demonstrate that you are hearing and valuing what is being shared. Responses might include comments like these:

- What does that look like?
- Can you give me an example?
- Wow, that's a totally new insight!

Procedural Safeguards

The principle of **procedural safeguards** ensures that the rights of students with disabilities and their parents are afforded protections related to special education processes and documentation. These protections include, but are not limited to, student records (i.e., right to review, attain copies, add statements) and confidentiality. Confidentiality must be assured in all matters pertaining to the identifiability and life circumstances of students being considered for, placed in, or receiving special education services.

Challenges—Challenges unique to CLD students include the ad hoc or random solicitation of translators to facilitate sensitive conversations. It is unfortunately still commonplace to hear about school-based paraprofessionals or other unqualified, unrelated adults used to facilitate communication around due process.

Caveats—As with all students, families have networks of relationships and interactions outside of school that may intertwine with staff and other students or their parents. It is simply good practice to treat all others with respect, be discreet when discussing sensitive issues with and about students and families, and keep confidentiality a top priority.

Considerations—Personnel trained in the verbiage and intent of IDEA, who also possess the interpersonal, linguistic, and social skills to mediate communications, will exponentially benefit all involved in the process. The following questions can support reflection on procedural safeguards currently in place:

- What types of services are employed to assure parental access to documents created for special education processes?

- Is the language of the interpreter service (phone, in-person, internet) comprehensible to the family?
- Does the interpreter or interpreter service employed understand the intent of special education processes and terminology?
- Are the personnel who are relied upon for verbal or document translation trained in the principles of confidentiality for students with disabilities and their families?

RESPONSE TO INTERVENTION: MOVING BEYOND REDUCTIONISTIC EXERCISES

The 2004 reauthorization of IDEA sought to address some of the challenges that were faced by teachers and parents in the identification and placement of CLD populations. For the first time, an approach by professional experts in special education was promoted that was more individualized and centered on addressing the academic challenges the CLD student was facing by providing **multitiered systems of support (MTSS)**. The reauthorization permitted (1) demonstration of continued poor performance when the student is provided with a research-based intervention and (2) conducting an assessment to demonstrate a pattern of strengths and weaknesses, which could include ability–achievement discrepancy (PL 108-446, Part B, Sec 614(b)(6)(b)). The 2004 federal provision also allowed for **response to intervention (RTI)** to be used as part of the specific learning disabilities (SLD) identification process.

Today, many education professionals recognize that RTI involves universal screening, evidence-based instructional programming and curricula, routine progress monitoring of all students, increasingly intensive supplemental support and intervention for struggling learners, and effective teaming practices. RTI provides an alternative to the traditional practices that have been employed in many schools in the past to support students who experience academic difficulties (Hamayan et al., 2013). It is a process of evidence-based research interventions used by educators in three tiers to monitor academic skills and determine students' academic performance.

Tier 1 focuses on providing all learners with the opportunity to excel in grade-level curricula, based on their potential, by receiving instruction that attends to their socioemotional, linguistic, cognitive, and academic needs by planning and delivering instruction that understands and maximizes the potential of the community of learners in the classroom. Universal screening is used to identify students who are at risk for school failure. These are quick probes, administered to assess all students' readiness for, or progress with, specific skills. Concern arises, however, when the "universal" metric assumes "universal" experience. We must consider this: Is the screening tool understood well enough that educators know how to triangulate tasks with indicators and examples of evidence outside the canned assessment?

Tier 2 is designed to provide the learner who is not successful in Tier 1 with more specific strategies that target the particular challenges the student may be experiencing during instruction. The goal is to observe the difficulties the learner may be experiencing and respond by using specific strategies that will offer additional support. The teacher's responsibility is to document the progress made by the learner to assess the effectiveness of the more targeted intervention that has been specifically designed for the student. A more formal definition according to the National Center on Response to Intervention (NCRTI) (2010) is as follows:

> Secondary prevention typically involves small-group instruction that relies on evidence-based interventions that specify the instructional procedures, duration (typically 10 to 15 weeks of 20- to 40-minute sessions), and frequency (3 or 4 times per week) of instruction. Secondary prevention has at least three distinguishing characteristics: it is evidence-based (rather than research-based); it relies entirely on adult-led small-group instruction rather than whole-class instruction; and it involves a clearly articulated, validated intervention, which should be adhered to with fidelity. (p. 10)

Providing high-quality instruction in Tier 1 and Tier 2 intervention that is more focused on the specific needs of the learner may be the additional boost the student needs to reach the grade-level academic goals. But what if this is not the case? What next?

Students who do not make the expected growth in Tier 1 and Tier 2 are provided with more intensive interventions that further address the challenges they are facing in a one-on-one setting. Here is how NCRTI (2010) defines Tier 3 intensive intervention:

> Tertiary prevention, the third level of the RTI prevention framework, is the most intensive of the three levels and is individualized to target each student's area(s) of need. At the tertiary level, the teacher begins with a more intensive version of the intervention program used in secondary prevention (e.g., longer sessions, smaller group size, more frequent sessions). However, the teacher does not presume it will meet the student's needs. Instead, the teacher conducts frequent progress monitoring (i.e., at least weekly) with each student. (p. 11)

In Tier 3, educators continue with progress monitoring of the learner's response to the intervention to determine whether, and to what degree, it is helping the student and then adjust the intervention accordingly. If the student has not shown academic growth, and findings align with other sources of information (e.g., child study team reports, parent/guardian input), these data can be useful in determining eligibility for special education services.

Although RTI is an alternative practice before referring students for special education evaluation, "the identification, assessment, and placement of students into such categories are problematic on all counts, and especially so when the students are ELLs" (Hamayan et al., 2013, p. 57). Figure 2.1 provides a cursory introduction to the challenges, caveats, and considerations for RTI in practice when the population that is served is culturally and linguistically diverse. Given these concerns, how is it that intervention processes *implemented correctly* can benefit all students by providing timely support, appropriate interventions, and culturally and linguistically responsive pedagogy?

Disconnects arise when we lose sight of the potential for RTI to inform systems, and when methods used to measure "response" are considered more reflective of students' capacities than the appropriateness of instructional design. How often are school rankings on tests attributed to students or

Figure 2.1. A Biography-Driven Perspective on RTI: Three Cs to Moving Forward With RTI

Challenges	Caveats	Considerations/Calibrations
• Core instruction	• "Core" may be misinterpreted as a place rather than access to full participation in the core curriculum, along with peers.	• Do the students assigned to a back table with a paraprofessional for a different activity receive the same amount of core instruction as class peers?
• Interpretation of RTI	• Are there indications that RTI (or similar intervention model) is considered the path to special education? Is there a sense that paperwork around these processes is just "a hoop to jump through" or forms to complete to "get a student tested for SPED"? • Tiers may not be fluid "spot treatments" to address skill needs. • Nonresponders may be moved to more intensive tiers without discussion around the appropriateness of the instructional methods or means of assessment, leading to conclusions that problems are situated in the student.	• Identify system or site personnel capable of clarifying and supporting the purpose of RTI. • Does data demonstrate that students' assignments to groups and interventions vary by curricular demand? • Does data indicate that tiered instruction *as designed and implemented* addresses the identified need for skill development? If not, why? • How frequently does our district review data for the purposes of evaluating adopted methods and materials?

Figure 2.1. (*Continued*)

Challenges	Caveats	Considerations/Calibrations
• Assumptions around the universality of screeners	• Are screening tools measuring what they purport to measure? • Do those involved in data discussion understand the rationales and assumptions underlying each measure? • Can those involved explain *why* we measure *what* and *how* we can sample similar pathways in students with differing linguistic experience (e.g., Does decoding speed correlate to reading comprehension the same way for English learners as for those who make instantaneous meaning of decoded words because English is their native language?)	• Identify ways a teacher can "look for" or "listen for" skills demonstrated during activities, play, and instruction (i.e. BDI) outside of the formal screener. • Develop additional means to assess specific skills probed by screeners when not demonstrated by the "universal" probe. For example, words harvested from the student's own use of the target language (i.e. English) will improve that student's ability to hold words in mind while performing tasks such as sound blending/manipulation, decoding new patterns, spelling, etc.
• Use of RTI data to support eligibility for specific learning disabilities	• Data representing student response to instruction and/or materials that presume all students have the same experiential and linguistic backgrounds are not valid indicators of student capacities to learn on par with peers.	• Use of biography-driven approaches and interventions allow teams greater confidence in statements around the appropriateness of instruction. In addition, such methods permit greater confidence in the determination of disability, while also providing essential information necessary to develop IEPs where indicated.
• Reliance on standardized assessments to diagnose student learning problems	• Waiting for test results to make decisions around need may deny students' access to FAPE. • Standardized tests may be invalid or unreliable for the individual student. • Single measures and point-in-time assessments are subject to numerous variables related to the persons, interaction dynamics, and appropriateness of the test/task.	• Interventions and processes that yield rich yet refined information related to students' assets and needs allow informed professionals to carefully select among or adapt tasks or probes necessary to triangulate findings across settings, including the perceptions of teachers and families.
• Disregard for, or misunderstanding of, CLD students' language biography	• CLD students bring diverse language experience to school. Unless a student is solely, formally, and recently educated in another country, tests normed using the language of that country will not be reliable alternatives to problematic interpretation of English-only tests or probes. • Bilingual CLD students may present as less fluent or even language impaired when compared with monolinguals of either language. • CLD students may be receptively bilingual/multilingual (comprehending aspects of 2+ languages) while preferring to speak only one language. This often occurs with students who have diminished opportunities to speak the home language upon entry to English-only or English-speaker-majority schools.	• Student language skills are best considered an interacting system of language capacities that the student can draw upon (or be hindered in that regard) for purposes of communication in varying contexts, acquiring and transmitting information, and converting ideas to print. • Instructional methods that recognize and harvest (otherwise untapped) knowledge eliminate the need for teachers to assume, predetermine, or inadvertently block students' access to their full complement of skills.

Critical Question: Do my assessment methods provide information about *how a student learns,* rather than whether they pass the test?

community versus a mismatch between them and the adopted (often marketed) methods of teaching and assessment? Claims of "evidence-based" programs or products frequently rely on reductive conclusions about, and marginal inclusion of, students with cultural and linguistic diversity—if CLD learners are considered at all.

Question to Consider

Tier 2 is fluid, with the expectation that students will move in and out of this level of support as needs arise and are responsively and responsibly met. In what ways might strict adherence to protocols for intervention blind us to student skills that could more readily bridge to core success than the scripted programs or texts recommended for this tier?

Voices From the Field

Introducing our special education teachers to biography-driven instruction (BDI) brought forth an urgency to create effective, responsive classrooms where their students' assets became central to planning and collaborating. These efforts alleviated the disconnect between the students' disabilities and the opportunities they were provided to be part of the classroom community. With increased attention to the knowledge, experiences, and skills that students brought with them, the teachers also were better prepared to address their linguistic needs.

—Martha Mendoza, Elementary School Principal

It is beyond the scope of this book to address all instructional and assessment considerations for emergent bilingual learners. These topics are treated in more extensive detail elsewhere (e.g., Herrera, 2022; Herrera, Cabral, & Murry, 2020; Herrera & Murry, 2016). However, as introduced in Chapter 1, the chapters that follow provide a theoretical and practical framework for educators seeking to respond to the challenges and caveats of both IDEA and MTSS/RTI in a more culturally responsive and sustaining way, through an approach that situates the biography of the learner as central to planning and instruction.

BIOGRAPHY: NOTICING AND DOCUMENTING LEARNER POTENTIAL

Thus far, this chapter has provided a broad-stroke reminder of how systems frame equity in ensuring that every learner is provided with the highest quality education possible. Chapter 1 detailed the ongoing challenges that have been raised in the field of special education for decades as researchers and practitioners have grappled with the impact of policy and practice on emergent bilingual learners. Often for educators, the policy and theory are difficult to actualize in classrooms where the diversity is such that it often seems impossible to provide Tier 1 instruction that would address the range of language proficiencies, life experiences, academic variance, and differential pace of cognitive processing that occurs within any lesson. Coupled with the sociopolitical demands for continuous testing and adhering to procedures that ensure equal treatment for all, these and many other reasons contribute to educators falling back into "one size fits all" interventions in an effort to take the path that will do the least harm to the learner.

In Chapter 1, the core theoretical tenets of this work were discussed in relation to creating an ecology within classrooms that has the potential to strengthen cognitive and socioemotional resilience. Cognitive resilience is a learner's ability to move beyond the perceived feelings of inadequacy and nonacceptance and cognitive belief systems that impact cognitive functioning and learning (Staal et al., 2008). According to Hammond (2015), cognition and learning are interrelated, and feelings of academic failure or lack of acceptance by peers may lead CLD students to not achieve their full potential. Similarly, socioemotional resilience reflects the learner's positive psychosocial adjustment despite factors that pose a risk to well-being (e.g., low socioemotional support, low expectations for learning, low assumptions of potential) (Haft et al., 2016; Herrera, 2022).

Through BDI, educators facilitate engagement and learning that has the potential to promote students' cognitive and socioemotional resilience. By setting conditions and monitoring situations mediated through the biography of the learner, and by utilizing strategies that support cognitive engagement, learners who experience authentic *cariño* from the teacher and their peers engage in and take ownership of their learning, adjusting to the cognitive and social demands of the lesson. The goal in BDI is for educators to become aware of the ecology of the classroom in relation to the community of learners and to monitor students' cognitive processes and states of mind in order to foster academic access for *all* learners.

Teachers who plan with specific cognitive, metacognitive, and social/affective strategies in mind are flexible, individualize instruction, and create social opportunities for talk. The student biography drives learning beyond the diagnosis and defines the learner based on their potential rather than a label. Situationally, the teacher observes states of mind and other factors that may inhibit learning. Effective instruction with CLD students involves seeing the challenges a learner is facing and then adjusting, supporting, and documenting the conditions that promote the resilience and success not only of the individual, but also the classroom community.

In Chapters 3–5, educators are guided through fundamental considerations in planning and delivering instruction that informs decision-making through a lens of authentic production and assessment. Assessment of student performance grounded in an understanding of the learner from an asset-driven perspective allows for documenting the cognitive and social resilience of the learner when certain conditions are present. Although more traditional data can serve as indicators in decision-making related to instruction and interventions within RTI, the power of what a learner can do is bound by the context and conditions that are planned for and created by the teacher, based on who the community of learners are and what the teacher believes is possible for that population. The cognitive processes of all learners are strengthened when educators move beyond data and teach by using multiple forms of engagement, representation, and expression that permit meaningful access to grade-level concepts.

Biography-driven instruction seeks to highlight the role of the instructional process in relation to the principles of IDEA and RTI. Multiple strategies for assessment provide learners with opportunities to authentically demonstrate what they know and can do. When the degree of support necessary for student success exceeds what is available under the auspices of general education, *and* evidence across settings indicates the presence of innate barriers to learning, that student may be a candidate for special education. Referral for evaluation, however, is never precluded or promoted due to external factors such as prior educational experience, years of residence, or presumption that special education services benefit "any" student. As detailed in Chapter 8, nonexceptional learners are more likely to experience cognitive, linguistic, social, and academic harm when placed in programming for disabled learners.

CONCLUSION

Educators must integrate data-informed practices in ways that optimize teaching time, produce evidence of what learners know and can do (and under what conditions), and maximize holistic outcomes for learners. Inclusive classrooms that build on students' assets provide the basis for biography-informed interventions and supports that respond to the culturally and linguistically influenced realities of learners and their families. Transforming expectations, perspectives, and practices surrounding core instruction, tiered supports, and special education processes (e.g., referral, evaluation, placement, and services) is key to ensuring that instruction is responsive to learners' assets and needs, and that the principles of IDEA undergird our actions. Under such conditions, *all learners*, especially those who are culturally and linguistically diverse, will experience increasingly equitable opportunities to learn and an enriched academic life.

CHAPTER 2 QUESTIONS FOR REFLECTION AND DISCUSSION

As educators, the first step toward undoing, rethinking, and reimagining is to reflect upon the three C's—challenges, caveats, and considerations—that impact our practices. As professionals in a field that has so many competing agendas, it is critical to reflect upon about our views and perspectives and the role we play in making a difference in the lives of students and families. Reflect on this chapter and independently or collectively with a team, take a position on how you would respond to the following questions.

Challenges

1. How might challenges to alignment with IDEA be impacted by systems and individual-level mindsets?
2. What aspects of your own training and experience have provided you the greatest insight to the principles underlying compliance requirements?

Caveats

1. What influences do structural- or system-level resources have on compliance with the spirit of IDEA for CLD students?
2. How might disconnects in the provision of supports, or interpretation of results gathered, during the RTI process misdirect the path to evaluation and placement for CLD students in your setting?

Considerations

1. In what ways does awareness of the principles informing IDEA add to your consideration of instructional *practice* as a vital metric of compliance?
2. How might your insights and conversations around the principles of IDEA leverage change in practice in your classroom, school, or district?

Part II

APPLYING BIOGRAPHY-DRIVEN PRACTICES IN INCLUSIVE CLASSROOMS

A Biography-Driven Individualized Educational Plan

I have marveled at how much my culturally and linguistically diverse learners can do when I plan and deliver instruction that centers their language, culture, and experiences when I teach. You know I really wasn't into biography; we have had so much training on accepting different cultures that I guess in many ways I was over it all. I guess what has most surprised me, when you see them for their potential, instead of what is on the IEP (you do use that as a baseline/plan) is how much more they can do than I would expect based on their disability. Goes to show that we can never predict what a student can and cannot produce when you provide an opportunity for them to just be without a label hanging over their head.

—Elementary Teacher, Anonymous

In education, without a doubt, we are guided by the politics and policy of the day. Most often these agendas/guides are founded within a "policy and science" perspective, that is, the result of research and legislation to ensure that empirical evidence supports the actions of educators practicing their craft and that all students have equitable educational opportunities. As you have already read in this book, this holds especially true for CLD learners who have been labeled with a learning disability. For years, the question has revolved around "Is it language or learning disability?" Often, educators, fearing that they are not prepared to meet the needs of emergent bilingual learners, will turn to special education with the good intention of allowing the learner to receive more attention for their "gaps" and believing that much of what has been observed in the classroom is consistent with behaviors that are present across a range of disabilities. Furthermore, as well-intentioned teachers gather and prepare to refer the CLD learner for testing, given the lack of training in this area, they are unprepared to recognize that instruction does not always meet the linguistic, cultural, and cognitive needs of the learner being referred. Once placed in special education, learners are labeled and their true learning needs continue to go unmet, while their new placement creates a range of new challenges rooted in inequitable access to the grade-level, standards-based curriculum and the academic interactions with peers that are needed to foster language, literacy, and academic development.

Framing the issue around the Individuals With Disabilities Education Act (IDEA) (2004), which provides guidance on the rights of the learner and the responsibility of the school and their educators, the process for answering the question of appropriate programming often begins with the goal that a CLD learner should be placed in the setting that is the "most accommodating," to provide them with the necessary support systems that will increase their social and academic success. Although educators might all agree that this is the goal, the process fails to account for the realities of bilingual/multilingual learners. According to Nganga (2015), our systems do not have policies and procedures with clear expectations that have been normed for the populations they represent. The sociocultural, linguistic, and cognitive dimensions of the learner are neither considered nor valued within the processes set forth for referring or serving CLD students and families. Much of what is asked in schools by educators is static and rote. Absent is a deeper delving into the history of the family and the learner—a documentation of the funds of knowledge, those assets that are bound by the familiar, and the knowledge that is accumulated over decades of living in a culture surrounded by language and wrapped in shared ways of being, valuing, knowing, and doing. Knowing what is important to ask requires us first to briefly rewind and review what has been covered thus far in the previous chapters.

As discussed in Chapter 2, IDEA (2004) details six important principles for us to consider. However, in schools and classrooms across the country, there frequently is a disconnect between the *intent* of the law and the policies that follow it. How it is implemented can differ from school to school, often depending on the population served and the need for efficiency in placement. Little consideration is given to the biography of the CLD family or learner regarding how assessments are being interpreted for placement and programming, or how instructional practices may negatively impact the academic trajectory of the learner. Researchers (e.g., Artiles et al., 2002; Baca & Cervantes, 1991) have determined that for many CLD learners, placement in a special education classroom led to regression in learning, as CLD students often took on the behaviors of their peers. The effect had a long-lasting and consequential negative impact on the learner's social and academic trajectory.

This chapter attempts to illustrate how teachers can navigate instructional processes, based on where the learner is on the continuum of prereferral for testing, referral, and IEP monitoring to ensure that all CLD learners experience access, engagement, and hope. The chapter will focus on what considerations and actions are necessary for delving deeper into framing all instruction with the biography of the learner in mind, and scaffolding teaching for both social and academic success. We will explore this culturally and linguistically responsive approach to education by first uncovering, documenting, and understanding the learner's biopsychosocial history—in other words, who the learner is, based on all human experience, including culture, language, cognition, and responses to sociopolitical factors. We will undertake this exploration from a sociocultural, linguistic, and cognitive point of view, with a focus on creating an ecology that represents, respects, and intertwines that history into the daily instructional and social practices of the classroom.

MOVING BEYOND GOOD INTENTIONS TOWARD DOCUMENTABLE IMPACT

Instruction that is guided by the assets of the learner's family and community requires the teacher to (1) be informed by the knowledge that has been uncovered and documented about those assets, (2) determine how instruction will be guided by that knowledge, and (3) make decisions about how that knowledge will be documented and affirmed. Research has long demonstrated the *why* of grounding all our educational action in response to the community, family, and learner (e.g., Gay, 2000; Moll et al., 1992; Nieto, 1992; Paris, 2012). Yet, a "one size fits all" approach continues to guide and inform assessment and practice. Recent studies (Reyes, 2022; Steen, 2022) have found that many of the educators and teams who referred, observed, evaluated, and placed CLD students had little training in moving beyond expected protocols for evaluation and differentiation of instruction. These researchers found that even in those instances when the team has developed protocols, the procedural nature of the process pays little attention to considerations that are relevant for assessing CLD students. Such findings represent a call to action.

Our classrooms will always represent a microcosm of the society in which we live. Undoubtedly, we will find learners who live at very different places along the cultural, linguistic, cognitive, and socioemotional continua. It would be impossible to document with any single instrument the assets, strengths, weaknesses, and gaps learners bring to the learning context. When we combine this complex picture with the additional sociopolitical dynamics (e.g., national, state, and local sociopolitical environments), we quickly realize that intent is not enough. As educators, our profession has called upon us to be critically reflective thinkers who ask questions and who bend and shape instruction to push back against agendas that do not benefit families and communities. Our intent must move toward action that is driven by recognizing that both core instruction and planned interventions must be contextualized within the histories of the family and the learner. In Chapter 1 we addressed the impact that IDEA had on students of color and the negative consequences of not addressing the challenges and threats that are present in schools and classrooms. We now begin to explore pathways and actions that can be taken in practice to protect the rights of CLD learners while maintaining the intent of IDEA to ensure equity in assessment and learning for all students.

Community, Home, and Biography as Points of Departure

Moll and colleagues (1992) have long posited that learners and their families possess what they termed "funds of knowledge," that is, ways of knowing and doing that comprise the strategic knowledge of the household. Learners also benefit from heritage practices, the wealth of knowledge passed on from generation to generation among those who share similar ethnic roots, and from community practices, which often reflect new, dynamic, and hybrid ways of knowing, communicating, and doing that sustain learners (Alim & Paris, 2017). Regardless of ethnicity or language, all CLD learners are part of communities that are rooted in their language, traditions, knowledge, and ways of doing. It also must be understood that within groups, families live and breathe their own sociocultural and linguistic journey, based on sociopolitical and personal narratives that evolve from generation to generation, based on place and time, as they acculturate or assimilate to their surroundings.

Although there are many shared characteristics of CLD families, we must also listen for and respond to the personal history and narrative of the individual family. These shifts require educational systems to put processes into place that prepare educators to understand the nuances and uniqueness of every family and child. As the conversation and struggle continue in the field of special education surrounding over/underrepresentation of CLD populations, core instruction is increasingly recognized as a pivotal time to allow for more informed decisions to be made related to instruction and assessment both for learners referred for evaluation and for those who are receiving services. Maximizing core instruction requires us to shift our lens from identifying and documenting/confirming perceived deficits, toward investigating and leveraging assets. Core instruction then becomes a space in which we explore what learners *can do* from multiple angles in order to identify conditions that are most effective for turning resting/latent potential into documentable gains.

Seeing the Learner Through a Prism of Possibilities

Understanding the interconnectedness of sociocultural, linguistic, cognitive, and academic dimensions and how they support students in finding their place within a classroom ecology is critical for planning and delivering instruction and conducting assessment that is responsive to the CLD learner (Herrera, 2022; Herrera, Cabral, & Murry, 2020). As human beings, from the time we are born we take our behavioral, learning, language, and socioemotional cues from others (Haught & McCafferty, 2008; Lantolf & Poehner, 2008). We present as learners ready to process information and use language in the ways we have been socialized within our community and family. Understanding the **sociocultural dimension** encompasses observing and listening to the learner's idiosyncratic ways of expressing, processing, and behaving. Aspects of the learner's identity are manifested in subtle ways as they produce through drawing, writing, and interacting with others and their surroundings.

Often teachers will say, "They are so off target, distracted, and withdrawn" when describing the CLD students whom they are referring for evaluation or learners receiving services. The first question to be asked is, Why? In what ways has instruction been planned to provide opportunities for learners to share what they know based on their socialization in a culture and language not represented in the typical curriculum. Understanding the role that the sociocultural dimension plays during a lesson has the potential to greatly inform our interpretation of a student's behavior, engagement, and use of language.

The **linguistic dimension** encompasses a learner's fluid use of language for different purposes and with different people. How language is used in communication for learning often differs based on context and the learner's socioemotional response to their teacher, peers, and other school personnel. Learners who experience socioculturally bound lessons within the safety of an identity-affirming classroom ecology draw from their full linguistic repertoire when they engage in learning. Think about the following exchange of ideas as students engage in a small-group conversation about a picture of a land formation in the center of a Linking Language poster (refer to Appendix A for a description of the Linking Language BDI strategy).

Sandra: . . . broken road.
Carmen: Yeah! (smiles and points to Sandra) Broken road.

Liz: (begins to write on the poster while teammates observe)

Miguel: (points to the poster) I gotta get it. I think this was caused by an earthquake.

Liz: I think. (writing)

Sandra: (points down at the poster) I see a lot of *espacio.*

Liz: Okay. (begins to write on poster)

Carmen: (wipes pencil eraser bits off the poster to make a cleaner space for Liz to write)

Liz: (bent over writing and speaking out loud) The (pauses) road (pauses again, this time waiting for the group to support)

Miguel: (points to place on poster where the writing should continue)

(Team begins to say each letter for Liz to write: "r," "o," "a".)

Carmen: (gestures to the poster with one hand and attempts to grab the pencil to erase part of the previous writing; when Liz keeps the pencil, Carmen indicates what to erase)

Carmen: Ahí dice "rock."

(Students laugh briefly.)

Sandra: That's an "a." (shifts around the table toward Liz to help, saying each letter with the Spanish pronunciation) *"r," "o," "a."*

Miguel: (repeating the Spanish name of the letter) *"a," "a," "a."*

Sandra: "d."

Liz: The road.

Miguel: (points to the poster) "d."

Sandra: Muy bien.

In this classroom, the teacher considered the context: Who in the community of learners would support and scaffold for the learner receiving services, and for English learners? Often, we limit or take away opportunities given our assumptions about the learner's potential based on a test score (e.g., English language proficiency assessment, academic screener, progress monitoring). When instruction instead is planned with the learner and the community in mind, the assets of each learner are used as scaffolds for entering conceptual learning and building language with peers based on the content. Language never ceases to be dynamic when students are engaging and

participating in the learning process, drawing from what they know in order to contribute. In this small-group conversation, the sum of all the voices allows for peer teaching and collective learning.

Earlier in Chapters 1 and 2, we introduced the concept of biography-focused instruction leading to cognitive resilience, that is, a CLD learner's ability to draw from personal strengths to access and make sense of language and academic content, anchoring it ever more deeply into permanent memory. As CLD learners draw upon their sociocultural/socioemotional and linguistic dimensions, they engage in creative ways of accessing the content and scaffolding their own learning using cognitive, metacognitive, and social/affective strategies (Chamot & O'Malley, 1994; Herrera & Murry, 2016). Biography-driven instruction supports development of the **cognitive dimension** by guiding students to become independent in the way they use their culture, language, and ways of knowing to engage in learning. Hammond (2015) discusses the difference between a dependent learner and independent learner, reminding educators that a teacher's responsibility in scaffolding instruction is to provide strategies that the learner can draw upon when accessing background knowledge from all systems (community, home, and school). It is through the practice and application of social/affective, metacognitive, and cognitive strategies that the learner experiences collaboration, thinks about their own pathways for doing, and uses tools in the hand to work with content and to take it to permanent memory (Herrera, 2022).

For students who have been referred for observation or assessment or who already are receiving services, an equitable path must be grounded within the sociocultural and linguistic dimensions by selecting strategies that make it possible for the teacher to harvest the words and thoughts produced by the individual learner. These words and ideas represent the assets the learner has available for processing difficult and abstract concepts. The context (e.g., who we are teaching) dictates the conditions (how we are teaching) necessary for the learner to thrive in the classroom. The teacher is charged with planning the lesson to address the biography of the learner and to intentionally and consistently support the learner in making connections to new content and language.

The **academic dimension**, the last dimension of the CLD student biography, explores the level of access that the learner has been provided in the learning environment. For students who have been referred for evaluation, it is important to consider what has been provided (or denied) to them based on their language proficiency, socioeconomic level, and culture. The teacher is instrumental in advocating for the CLD learner. It is without question that the teacher who plans for, interacts with, and observes the learner daily is the most powerful voice in countering test results that reflect only point-in-time snapshots of the learner. By observing and listening to students from an asset perspective, they can describe what the learner *is able* to do and explain why they may appear withdrawn, have difficulty processing, or exhibit behaviors not appropriate in school.

For students receiving services, the teacher must be knowledgeable about the 14 disability categories listed within IDEA. Although it is not within the scope of this text to discuss each category, Morgan (2020) relates that CLD students who receive services within grade-level or content classes are most often identified within *subjective* disability categories, such as emotional disability and intellectual disability. For this reason, as researchers and educators we like to think more about the biography and characteristics of the learner and the contextual factors that influence their lives. We consider the diagnostic label to be something that informs, but should not define, our expectations regarding the capacities and potential of the learner, especially if the conditions include the teacher guiding the learner to engage in their **zone of proximal development (ZPD)** (Vygotsky, 1978).

The ZPD refers to what the learner can do with the support of a more expert peer or an adult (Vygotsky, 1978). What we do as educators influences how much the learner will engage and learn. What we do with the context, how we set conditions to support the state of mind of the learner, when we choose to situationally attend to what is produced, and most importantly how we determine grouping configurations to foster a community of learners who see the potential of their peers—these all are pivotal factors that influence the amount of time that students spend learning within their ZPD. Ecologies that are rooted in learners' biographies and orchestrated by the social interactions of the community are spaces where each learner feels respected, accepted, and supported.

Where Learners and Labels Collide: The Biopsychosocial History and the IEP

History is a term easily understood as an area of study that helps us retell what has happened in the past. In a school setting, educators are encouraged to explore the **biopsychosocial history** of the learner by purposefully asking questions and considering the biological, psychological, and sociological aspects of their history (lived experiences) (Engel, 1977; Gates & Hutchinson, 2005; Herrera, 2022; Saleebey, 2001). These aspects reflect the most basic elements of human experience contextualized within an individual's life. Understanding the history of the learner who has been referred or is receiving services informs educators on assets they possess and challenges that have been present over the course of their lives. A student's experiences based on skin color, social situation, and disability have a powerful impact on both what the learner sees as their potential and what educators see as possibilities.

Culturally responsive teaching focuses on educators being attentive to the culture and the language of the student. What does that mean when the students served in schools today come from (1) the same ethnicity, but have lighter/darker skin colors, (2) the same country, but not the same regions, (3) the same culture, but different socioeconomic levels, (4) the same native language, but different regional dialects? The concept of the biopsychosocial history of the learner is critical to the work of culturally responsive teaching because it reminds us to think beyond considering only cognitive (processing) and academic (success in the classroom) factors to critically reflect on the impact of the history of the CLD family and student and how those histories will be interpreted by educators as learners make their way through the system.

Biography-driven instruction has focused on how the four dimensions of the learner and the biopsychosocial history unite to inform educators, providing windows into the assets of learners and families, as well as the challenges that have colored their experiences. The deeper understanding of families and learners that results makes it possible for educators to more accurately interpret a learner's production in the classroom, responses to interventions, and assessment results during the evaluation process. Because BDI naturally scaffolds grade-level content for learners receiving services (Holmes, 2022), teachers gain alternative information (e.g., through authentic formative assessments) that often provides a clearer idea of what the learner can do and helps pinpoint whether the challenges they are experiencing are due to lack of access to quality programming/teaching that accommodates their individual assets and learning needs.

As educators, we must balance procedural concerns with the humanity of the learner. Understanding the limitations of putting CLD learners in the box of an IEP allows us to think beyond and consider different angles of the learning process in order to make instructional decisions that better prepare all learners to not only reach but *own* their potential. The reality in schools and classrooms today is that exclusion based on "label" is as present as high-quality inclusionary practices. An audit/questions on how the CLD learner has been provided with or denied access to highly relevant and rigorous curriculum, teaching, interaction with grade-level peers, and emotional support as their learning is advanced has the potential to shed light on key areas for targeted attention.

Questions to Consider

Has instruction been comprehensible to learners? Has the environment been attentive to the learner's state of mind? Is the ecology full of positive energy/ buzz?

As the teacher plans for instruction, understanding how the CLD learner is perceived (e.g., an indigenous child who exhibits behaviors that do not align with the dominant culture) requires understanding how perceptions of skin color, language, ways of living, and emotions can impact the effectiveness of our instruction and perceptions of (and responses to) disability. By exploring the biopsychosocial history of the learner, educators can begin to understand how the external and internal dynamics of schooling may have real consequences for the ways learners are motivated (or not) to engage in learning and have a positive self-image of their academic potential.

As educators, if we entertain that a student's biography (sociocultural, linguistic, cognitive, and academic) must be relevant during core instruction for equity to exist, including for learners who are referred and those who are receiving services, then the time has come to move toward a culturally responsive and sustaining pedagogy that aligns with standards and utilizes the mandated curriculum, but also creates a classroom context that reflects and includes the learner's biography during the opening, work time, and closing of a lesson. It is in this way that instruction becomes responsive to the learner and creates equitable opportunities for engagement, motivation, and learning. The IEP does *not* provide us with a roadmap for this responsiveness to be part of our teaching. Instead, IEPs, current agendas, pacing, and assessment leave little time to humanize planning and delivery, especially if doing so is treated as an "add on." Without putting the learner at the center of our instructional efforts, equity will continue to be something we aspire to rather than a reality in our schools and classrooms.

An asset perspective enables us to understand the learner's unique point of departure and requires us to navigate and negotiate the IEP and the curriculum. In doing so, we consider factors that might impact classroom performance, including the following:

- What assumptions are held by the community, school, and family that have the potential for advancing or denying learning opportunities for the student based on their disability?
- How are assumptions about culturally and linguistically diverse learners addressed by educators?
- How may the IEP influence the opportunities afforded to the learner based on the unchecked assumptions about culture, language, and different ways of knowing and doing.
- How might bias in assessment (e.g., construction, norming, and/or interpretation of assessments) have influenced what is written in the plan?
- What questions have been raised about accommodations and interventions, including how they may conflict with or support the learner's language and culture?

Figure 3.1. Intersection of Biography, Biopsychosocial History, and Influencing Factors

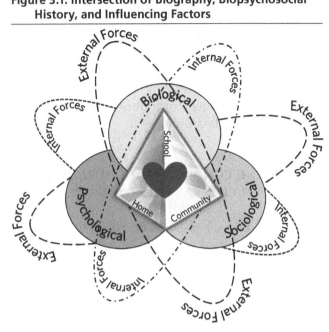

- What "tools in the hand" have been used to scaffold the learner's engagement and participation as an equal member of the community, regardless of (dis)ability, language, or cultural background?

Centering the biography and biopsychosocial history of the learner can transform and strengthen processes for referral/services, resulting in a more humanistic approach to meeting students' needs founded upon authentic *cariño* (Bartolomé, 2008; Herrera, Porter, & Barko-Alva, 2020; Valenzuela, 1999). Figure 3.1 illustrates intersections between a holistic, asset, and strengths-based perspective of the learner and the internal and external forces at play during decision-making on referrals for CLD learners and programming and instruction for exceptional learners.

REDEFINING POSSIBILITIES THROUGH EQUITABLE INSTRUCTIONAL DELIVERY

At the beginning of this chapter, we shared a teacher's reflection related to a student performing at a level far exceeding what was written in their IEP. As stated earlier in the Introduction, the

impetus for this book was the number of teachers who voiced the same surprise and excitement after delivering instruction that yielded evidence of a learner's increased engagement, production, and academic success. As educators, if we serve learners on IEPs, we are aware that the document often prepared by a team of knowledgeable educators is only a point of departure for ensuring that a learner's identified disability is addressed. Often the plan is reviewed only once or twice a year to ensure that the student is receiving the appropriate services. Imagine what happens in the many days and hours that the learner is receiving high-quality instruction. It may well be that what was planned may need to look different for the learner given the advances they have made after finding themselves part of a learning community that supports and accepts them.

Chapter 1 briefly discussed the conundrum and complexities of our decision-making for learners who are culturally and linguistically diverse, especially those who speak a language other than English and have been socialized in cultural contexts that do not match that of the educational system in which they find themselves. For these emergent bilingual learners, it is imperative that planning and instruction be culturally and linguistically responsive and guided by their biography. A teacher's biography-driven approach to instruction is informed by the assets and challenges of the four dimensions of the student biography, situated within the context of the learner's biopsychosocial history, with continual awareness of the sociopolitical dynamics of the day.

The phases of BDI instructional delivery that are briefly introduced in the following sections of this chapter seek to enhance teachers' capacities to create a classroom where core instruction is grounded in the enactment of culturally responsive and sustaining pedagogy (Alim & Paris, 2017; Gay, 2018). It is well documented that high-quality core instruction is necessary not only to accelerate language and academic achievement, but also to ensure that those students who are in the referral process or receiving services are provided the opportunity to demonstrate their knowledge, spirit, culture, and language—to make public the power that often lies dormant given scripted curricula written from a monocultural lens where the CLD learner finds little connection.

Gay (2018) explains that learners often are "taught from the middle-class Eurocentric frameworks that shape school practices" (p. 28). Critically reflecting on our perspectives helps ensure that our pedagogical practices reflect the ideals we hold for CLD students' learning. Educators can proactively assess their perspectives and instructional practices by doing the following (Herrera, 2022, p. 75):

- Considering the culture and sociopolitical climate of the school
- Exploring the visible environment and asking questions about what is invisible
- Viewing curriculum from a "student biography" perspective versus a "prescriptive response to learning" perspective
- Becoming informed about the myths and misconceptions that may have negatively influenced their expectations of CLD students
- Examining pedagogical perspectives for any indications of a deficit perspective (i.e., one that does not maximize learning by building on students' assets and documented potential)
- Noting whether (or to what degree) social interactions among students in the classroom are based on a mutual respect of student biographies, which results when each student understands that knowledge and learning are uniquely shaped by the multiple languages and cultures represented in the classroom

Culturally responsive educators plan for and integrate the native language, reflect on grouping configurations, create opportunities where there are no right or wrong answers, and provide learners with plentiful avenues for making schematic connections to the content. Each is key to the phases of BDI lesson delivery, which serve as the heart of the opening, work time, and closing portions of the lesson. Such actions are pivotal to planning for instruction that activates, connects, and informs practice that is bound by respect for the knowledge, culture, and language of learners and their families. Without harvesting the words, experiences, and knowledge that all individual community members bring and creating that third space where we can bridge into complex learning, we will continue to fail in meeting the needs of CLD learners, including students who are referred and those receiving services. It will be impossible to celebrate the possibilities and harvest learners' language, ideas, and personal connections (which sometimes can be private) if there is no evidence that such contributions will be valued in the school or classroom.

CREATING CONDITIONS AND SITUATIONS FOR CLD LEARNERS TO THRIVE

The phases of lesson delivery described in this chapter provide a canvas of opportunity for the learner and a new way for the teacher to assess learning using a much wider lens. Focused on what we know about how the brain processes information (Sousa, 2017) and the social nature of human learning and development (Vygotsky, 1978), these phases emphasize the role we play in ensuring that the foundations of culturally and linguistically responsive/sustaining pedagogy are present in our daily planning and delivery of instruction.

Activation Phase: I Remember When

Think about how often we say, "Remember when. . . ." We do this when we are in conversation with others, trying to help them connect with what we are saying or make sense of a difficult concept. The brain automatically seeks out patterns in the information we take in, in order to comprehend what we are learning (Bor, 2012). New information is learned only if it can be attached to something that is known or has meaning for the learner (Darling-Hammond et al., 2020). Students arrive in our classrooms with background knowledge (assets) that they have accumulated from home, community, and school. This background knowledge and how it is processed and shared provide the teacher with a "first look" into what the learner can do.

During the **activation phase** of the lesson, the teacher plans for the context (who is in the room) first and then the curriculum. In this phase, the teacher selects a strategy that will be used throughout the lesson to harvest the learner's words, observe for processing and connections the learner makes, and gain insight into what the learner knows before the lesson begins. The activation phase also serves to support the teacher in contextualizing the content through the students' biographies as the lesson unfolds. What becomes evident over the course of systematic and continuous use of the strategy during this phase is how the learner's strengths and challenges present themselves, providing critical information for the teacher on how the lesson should be orchestrated situationally during work time. Also evident is the self-confidence the learner gains when they realize there are no wrong or right answers, only an opportunity for entering learning.

During this time, the tool in the hand becomes a learning strategy, in that over time it can support the learner with social/affective, cognitive, and metacognitive moves that foster ownership and autonomy over the learning process. Figure 3.2 provides examples for each type of learning strategy. The BDI strategy tool is flexible and is used in real time to scaffold academic discourse, set the path for

Figure 3.2. Three Types of Learning Strategies

Strategy	Description	Definition
Metacognitive Strategies		
Planning		
Advance organization	Preview Skim Gist	Previewing the main ideas and concepts of a text; identifying the organizing principle
Organizational planning	Plan what to do	Planning how to accomplish the learning task; planning the parts and sequence of ideas to express
Selective attention	Listen or read selectively Scan Find specific information	Attending to key words, phrases, ideas, linguistic markers, and types of information
Self-management	Plan when, where, and how to study	Seeking or arranging the conditions that help one learn
Monitoring		
Monitoring comprehension	Think while listening Think while reading	Checking one's comprehension during listening or reading
Monitoring production	Think while speaking Think while writing	Checking one's oral or written production while it is taking place
Evaluating		
Self-assessment	Check back Keep a learning log Reflect on what you learned	Judging how well one has accomplished a learning task
Cognitive Strategies		
Resourcing	Use reference materials	Using reference materials such as dictionaries, encyclopedias, or textbooks
Grouping	Classify Construct graphic organizers	Classifying words, terminology, quantities, or concepts according to their attributes
Note-Taking	Take notes on idea maps, T-lists, etc.	Writing down key words and concepts in abbreviated verbal, graphic, or numerical form
Elaboration of Prior Knowledge	Use what you know Use background knowledge Make analogies	Relating new to known information and making personal associations

(*Continued*)

Figure 3.2. (*Continued*)

Strategy	Description	Definition
Cognitive Strategies		
Summarizing	Say or write the main idea	Making a mental, oral, or written summary of information gained from listening or reading
Deduction/Induction	Use a rule/Make a rule	Applying or figuring out rules to understand a concept or complete a learning task
Imagery	Visualize Make a picture	Using mental or real pictures to learn new information or solve a problem
Auditory Representation	Use your mental tape recorder Hear it again	Replaying mentally a word, phrase, or piece of information
Making Inferences	Use context clues Guess from context Predict	Using information in the text to guess meanings of new items or predict upcoming information
Social/Affective Strategies		
Questioning for Clarification	Ask questions	Getting additional explanation or verification from a teacher or other expert
Cooperation	Cooperate Work with classmates Coach each other	Working with peers to complete a task, pool information, solve a problem, get feedback
Self-Talk	Think positive!	Reducing anxiety by improving one's sense of competence

Source: Adapted from *The CALLA Handbook* (1st ed., Table 4.1, pp. 62–63), 1994, by A. U. Chamot & J. M. O'Malley. Reprinted by permission of Pearson Education, Inc.

what is to come, and most importantly affirm the knowledge and relationships that emerge as the teacher encourages learners to make their cultural and linguistic dimensions an integral part of the lesson.

Reflect on the U-C-ME (Uncover, Concentrate, Monitor, Evaluate) strategy artifacts depicted in Figure 3.3. What can be gleaned about what the students know related to tropical islands? How could this information be used to bridge into the planned content and language of the lesson? What opportunity is afforded to CLD learners in the referral process and those receiving services?

Connection Phase: That Makes Sense to Me

Research on how the brain receives and processes information raises many questions about what the rhythm and pacing for high-quality instruction should sound and feel like in practice. Cognitive research has found that the human brain has roughly a 15- to 30-second holding pattern for new information (Weinstein, 2017). For the CLD learner, this time may be shorter depending on how the context

has been prepared to allow for their knowledge, culture, and native language to be affirmed and utilized in the learning space. If the brain is experiencing fear or sees no connection to the self, and if the new information is not context embedded and related to what was uncovered during the opening of the lesson, the information will disappear from memory long before it makes it to work time.

Utilizing the knowledge and associations documented during the activation phase, the teacher must now be prepared to bridge and make connections to the curricular content as the lesson moves deeper into addressing the language and content objectives. The teacher becomes the facilitator during work time to make the curriculum relevant by weaving in what is known and eliminating social threat. This sets up conditions for the learner to get ready to concentrate on the important information to be learned. In this way, the learner will be more readily able to articulate their views, engage in talk, and ultimately retain new information. As the learner uses the U-C-ME tool in the hand to strengthen their social/affective strategies (e.g., talk with peers, ask questions), cognitive strategies (ways of using tools

Figure 3.3. Activation Phase of U-C-ME

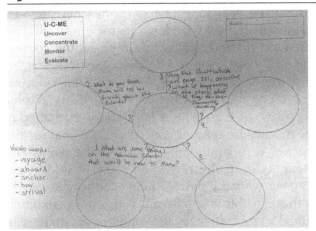

A 4th-grade teacher used the U-C-ME strategy to set conditions for all learners to activate the knowledge and ideas they brought to the text, which took place in a tropical island context. Students recorded words and images from their background knowledge in the center circle. The three close-up images of student artifacts illustrate that all learners were provided a risk-free opportunity to document their initial thoughts.

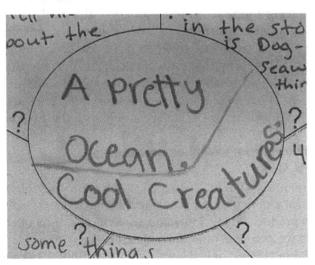

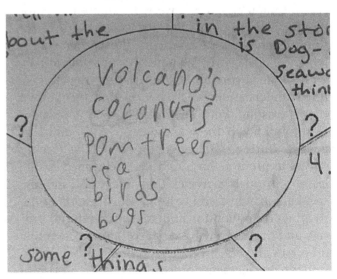

to remember), and metacognitive strategies (ways of using tools to reflect on the learning process), teachers begin to hear, "That makes sense to me."

When information begins to make sense to the brain, there is an increased likelihood that concepts will be retained in permanent memory (Sousa, 2017). In classrooms that are culturally responsive and biography-driven, the teacher facilitates learning and creates conditions that encourage students to practice and apply new concepts and vocabulary in interactive and meaningful ways. Multiple meaningful exposures for a variety of purposes and with different people are needed for learners to develop a thorough understanding and take ownership of the new language and concepts (Herrera, 2022).

The **connection phase** requires the teacher to navigate the four dimensions of the learners' biographies by supporting them in using their *selective attention* (looking for what is important) to make connections between the curriculum and the schemas that are available to them. The teacher observes and documents what the community and individual students are producing and revoices to weave together the individual student's words and ideas, those of their peers, and the curriculum. Important to this phase is the intentional and systematic use of grouping configurations that will support students to build confidence, recognize the value of their words and knowledge for achieving academic success, and become independent learners.

In Chapters 4 and 5, we will explore joint productive activity (JPA) and instructional conversation (IC) and how each supports the learner as they work collectively, collaboratively, and individually with the new content and language to develop refined understandings, always relating the known (their existing knowledge, skills, and language) to the unknown (new knowledge, skills, and language). During the connection phase, the teacher strives to promote both rigor and relevance during lessons through activities that integrate listening, speaking, reading, and writing. All educators in the room work to monitor students in the referral process and those receiving services to assess cognitive processes and affective filters in order to determine student engagement, processing of new information, state of mind, and learning outcomes.

The U-C-ME strategy sets the conditions for the teacher to model and guide students in using learning strategies. After they have activated, discussed, and documented their background knowledge during the activation phase, the teacher provides questions and asks students to use their selective attention to focus and concentrate on the content they will be reading and discussing with their peers after key information is provided. During the connection phase, the learner uses the U-C-ME graphic organizer to engage in a continuous exchange of ideas with the teacher and peers. The goal for the teacher is to continually return to the words and thoughts from the activation stage to bridge and connect with the new content. The teacher works with the whole group, small groups/pairs, and individual learners to make the content and language of the text accessible, as the learners use all available resources to answer the questions independently and collectively. The U-C-ME strategy asks students to be present in their learning by *monitoring* their understanding as they develop answers to the questions. Teachers remind students that, as we read, we keep the questions in mind, returning to our tool to remind ourselves of what is most important and to discuss ideas with our peers to support our learning, elicit additional connections, and document new ideas. Learners are encouraged to ask questions of one another to clarify their understanding of the vocabulary, topic, concepts, skills, and processes. Figure 3.4 highlights student work artifacts generated by 4th-grade learners using the U-C-ME strategy to document their responses to the text during the connection phase. When students have a tool to record their learning in progress, the teacher has ongoing opportunities to observe how students are making sense of the concepts, text, and key vocabulary. This formative assessment yields insights that enable the teacher to make situational decisions about how to scaffold, stretch thinking, and foster students' learning in collaboration with their peers.

Affirmation: I Will Remember This

The most vulnerable students in our classrooms often have a difficult time believing they have the capacity to produce linguistically and academically. How often do we as researchers and educators hear students say, "I don't know" or look away when questions are asked in a whole-group setting, attempting to avoid answering. One of the most heartbreaking experiences as an educator is when a community shuns a learner who does not "fit the mold" or does not communicate or

Figure 3.4. Connection Phase of U-C-ME

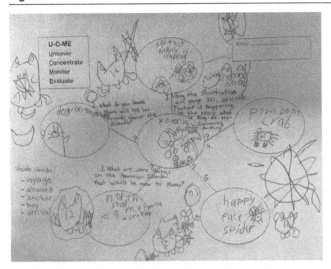
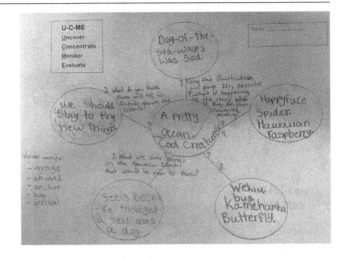
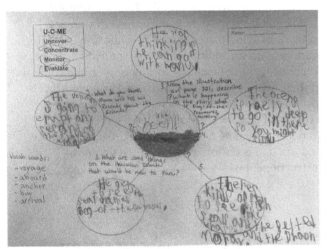

The teacher provided the class with three focal questions to consider as they read: 1) What are some things on the Hawaiian Islands that would be new to Manu? 2) What do you think Manu will tell his friends about the islands? 3) Using the illustration on page 321, describe what is happening in the story. What is Dog-of-the-Seawaves thinking?

As they read, students recorded answers to each of the questions in the corresponding ovals at the end of the spokes. The U-C-ME template served as a tool in the hand to scaffold learners' comprehension and discussion throughout the lesson.

behave according to socially imposed norms. In culturally and linguistically responsive settings, the goal is for all learners to be treated as equal members of the learning community. When respecting differences and valuing learners for who they are and what they *can* do are the norms, positive community dynamics become a reality. Students then feel free to produce at their own individual level, and from their own unique perspective. The tool in the hand illustrates for them and others that they *are* capable.

In BDI, it is critical that the teacher close the lesson by affirming growth and celebrating what was produced. In this **affirmation phase**, the words and ideas that have been affirmed incrementally throughout the lesson are now celebrated as a product that has been independently and collectively created. You may be thinking, "I already do that!" The difference in BDI is that the tool in the hand represents in a tangible form

the cognitive processing the learner has navigated and negotiated as the lesson unfolded. Both teachers and students are able to compare what was known against what was learned. How the community supported (or at times might have hindered) academic advancement is noted, as the class reflects on the learning process that took place and plans forward.

When CLD learners have been provided with a linguistic and academic scaffold, they are better able to assess their growth and see concrete evidence of academic success. They know that what they produced may not look like other students' products; however, they recognize that they were on the same road, producing at their potential. When we talk about relationship building, respect, and trust, this is where it begins. By preparing students to monitor and evaluate their own growth, they become increasingly comfortable with taking risks, knowing that their processing is

Figure 3.5. Affirmation Phase of U-C-ME

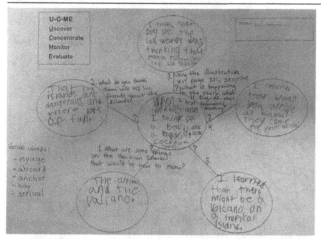

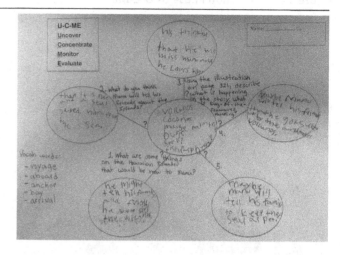

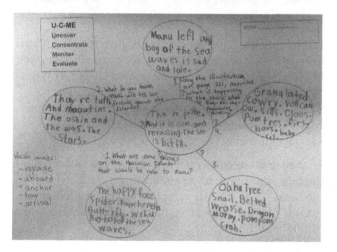

After reading the text, the students were asked to use the remaining two circles on the U-C-ME template to document things they had learned. This process fostered individual accountability while also providing learners with an additional level of individual choice. Students had the flexibility to engage with the content at their own linguistic, cognitive, and academic levels, given their unique points of departure. All means of expression (e.g., words, drawings) were valued. The students were able to refer to their U-C-ME template and use it as a resource when completing post-instructional tasks.

uniquely their own and that communication happens using multiple ways of showing, including writing, drawing, performing, and voicing knowledge.

As the lesson progresses with the U-C-ME strategy, the teacher takes time to guide the students to *evaluate* their progress by releasing them for partner or small-team talk. The teacher asks for evidence of how the question was answered. Did it come from what the teacher or peers shared? From the text or some other resource? How do learners know the answer is correct? Have they compared answers with their peers and discussed their findings? Teachers adapt the strategy to their needs as they provide learners with postinstructional tasks to summarize and demonstrate their learning. Observing U-C-ME in practice exemplifies what it means to have equity in a learning community. Figure 3.5 illustrates the individual outcomes for 4th-grade students who utilized U-C-ME to support their learning.

"MY TEACHER MADE ME SMART"

Consider the contextual and situational dynamics of the learning ecology captured in the following classroom experience.

Sitting at the back of the room, knowing the biographies of this beautiful community of very diverse learners, I observed how Ms. Luman orchestrated this group that had been identified by other teachers as "very difficult." I could see the energy she was expending on the learner who had been referred in order to create opportunities for engaging in context-embedded and low-risk work and then raising the bar to more context-reduced and cognitively challenging tasks. In the same way, she was partnering students whose language was not English with learners who would build on their words and value the native language. The flow of instruction was both strategic and standards-driven.

At the time of my observation, I became especially focused on one student, Sofia (pseudonym). She caught my attention, given her leadership and the emotional support she was giving the second-language learners. She helped them spell words, guided them to the correct page in the text, and affirmed them when they completed a task. She was keeping up with her own work while attending to others around her, not only her peers who were second-language learners but the whole group.

After the lesson, I approached Sofia and praised her on the support she had provided her peers and on how well she had performed. Eyes shining, she took it all in and left for recess. I was full of joy, as most of us are when we sit in a classroom where there is authentic cultural and linguistic support and exemplary instruction. I immediately shared with Ms. Luman how impressed I was with Sofia and what she was able to do, and I commented that learners like Sofia who were at grade level, socially accepted by all learners, and willing to engage would continue to make the world a better place. Ms. Luman looked at me and said thank you, but then shared that Sofia was one of her students who had a laundry list of labels. She explained that for the first time (as a 2nd-grader), Sofia was blossoming. Surprised, I asked if I could interview her after recess. When I talked with Sofia, I complimented her on how she was such a great peer and helped others, ending my conversation with, "Sofia, you are so smart!" She then turned to me and said, "Thank you! I used to be dumb, but now, my teacher made me smart!"

This simple statement from a beautiful, intelligent, and social 2nd-grader reminded me of the power we have as educators. When we see difference and disability, at times we fail to see the capacities and potential of the CLD learners we teach. As educators, our effectiveness is only as good as the observations, facilitation, and affirmation we provide all learners in our community.

TEACHERS WHO SEE, TEACHERS WHO KNOW: OBSERVATION, FACILITATION, AND AFFIRMATION

This chapter started by framing the four dimensions of the learner and exploring the biopsychosocial history and how it shapes and influences the learner's

biography. We encouraged consideration of questions such as: How do the background knowledge systems of the family and learner contribute to motivation, engagement, and learning during core instruction, when determining evaluation eligibility, and ultimately when we are providing services? How do educators move from preconceived ideas to planning and delivering instruction that is biography driven?

First and foremost, as educators we become involved in participatory activity, observing and engaging with students by listening and understanding from their frame of reference, always trying to understand how their thinking is culturally and linguistically bound and how their cognitive pathways may be influenced by their past experiences. We explore the experiences, language, and knowledge (assets) that the learner possesses so that we can responsively facilitate the learner to engage in their ZPD, taking them from the known to the unknown.

Scaffolding is essential for supporting each learner to engage and produce in the classroom. In BDI, scaffolding is about selecting "tools in the hand" that students can use to engage in learning. The teacher uses the tool for collecting and documenting both information and assets the learner brings (e.g., language, knowledge, experiences) that can be used to help them reach *their* potential. To make core (Tier 1) instruction accessible to all, it is critical to have a clear framework for collecting, documenting, and using the information to advance the learner socially, linguistically, and academically.

Drawing on the work of others (Davis, 2012; Doyle, 2011; Glasgrow & Hicks, 2009; Howe, 1999; Ormrod, 1995; Rodriguez et al., 2017), Gay (2018) summarizes many generally accepted principles of learning in the following way:

- Students' existing knowledge is the best starting point for the introduction of new knowledge (principle of similarity).
- Prior success breeds subsequent effort and success (principle of efficacy).
- New knowledge is learned more easily and retained longer when it is connected to prior knowledge, frames of reference, or cognitive schemata (principle of congruity).
- Reducing the "strangeness" of new knowledge and the concomitant "threat of the unfamiliar" increases students'

engagement with and mastery of learning tasks (principle of familiarity).

- Organizational and structural factors surrounding how one goes about learning have more powerful effects on the mastery of new knowledge than the amount of prior knowledge one possesses per se (principle of transactionalism).
- Understanding how students' knowledge is organized and interrelated—their cognitive structures—is essential to maximizing their classroom learning (principle of cognitive mapping).
- Expectations and mediations affect performance. If students think they can learn, and receive competent assistance from supporters (e.g., teachers, parents, peers, and other mentors) in the process, they will learn (principle of confidence and efficacy).
- School achievement is always more than academics. Invariably, learning takes place in context, and is influenced by the affective and caring climates of the places or settings where its efforts occur. The social, physical, emotional, psychological, cultural, political, and ethical dispositions, developments, and experiences of the participants in the learning process are significant contributing factors and crucial targets for teaching (principle of holistic education).
- Out-of-school experiences matter, and are resources and filters for in-school learning. These "funds of knowledge, skill, and experience" are assets, building blocks, and leverage for subsequent learning (principle of scaffolding). (p. 204)

These principles, each of which is reflected in the BDI framework (Herrera, 2022), highlight the importance of contextualizing our instruction within learners' existing assets, knowledge, and frames of reference.

Core instruction is about our ability as educators to maximize what the learner knows, consider where they socially position themselves in our classrooms, and explore how they cognitively process information. All learning is socioculturally, linguistically, and cognitively bound. Effective Tier 1 instruction is about orchestrating all the feelings, words, experiences, and knowledge into

a high-interest story where all community members become writers, producers, and actors in their learning. In this type of ecology, the teacher only serves to pull together all the pieces and provide the needed encouragement. Through their own power, the learners grow and build on the knowledge already rooted in their lives and biographies. The shift is real when the standards and curriculum become the plan and the learning community breathes life into learning.

Voices From the Field

Biography-driven instruction is an awesome way to see growth in a classroom. We have to understand that all kids have needs; some of them meet all the criteria to get an IEP. The BDI strategies help all students. In this instructional classroom, you will not *see* the different needs in the group. When using the DOTS chart (ABC chart), every student is able to write the words they know. Next, they are able to talk to a partner, and then the class discussion begins. Every student knows something. This tool in the hand uses prior knowledge so the comprehension is activated. The Linking Language strategy uses pictures of the important vocabulary words. The students are divided into groups, and they each have a pen and label the pictures with what they think, feel, or see. This activity activates the prior knowledge in every student. These are just a few examples. There are many more BDI strategies that fit all teaching styles and learning preferences. Prior knowledge activates the learning in all students and helps their scores go up. Seeing this in action with fidelity has proven effective. All students need access to prior knowledge to grow their academic language to access the curriculum.

—Alicia Birney, K–5 SPED (Special Education) Teacher

BUILDING BLOCKS: EQUITY AND AUTHENTIC *CARIÑO*

The act of teaching equitably is about humanizing the space in which we carry out our craft. As educators, we hold so much power over the biopsychosocial history of the learner. We can choose to emphasize the "deficits," as data is always available to remind us of the gaps that exist for our learners, or we can choose to attend to learners' biographies and focus on the richness of their languages, cultures, and cognitive pathways.

How we structure the cycle of the lesson, the strategies we choose, and the way we orchestrate interaction say so much about the ecology of the classroom, where the learner will feel either accepted or rejected, supported or neglected, capable or incapable—in other words, *worthy* of existing in the space or not worthy. In Chapter 1, we introduced authentic *cariño* as central to our work. Bartolomé (2008) and Valenzuela (1999) remind us that teaching is, above all, an action of love and acceptance, which we demonstrate by acknowledging the power and strength that exists when we activate, connect, and affirm all potential. Understanding what learners know, and drawing that knowledge into existence in the public space of the classroom, allows us to teach, monitor, and evaluate from an asset-based perspective that supports each learner to shine their brightest. In other words, as researchers and educators we want every child to feel like U-C-ME.

CONCLUSION

An exploration of the four dimensions of the CLD student biography (sociocultural, linguistic, cognitive, and academic) opens the door for educators to critically reflect on how our current models for evaluation and providing services may be leaving out the most important information of all—the biography of the learner! These four dimensions intersect with the learner's biopsychosocial history, which influences the learner's engagement, motivation, and cognitive belief system. Utilizing the activation, connection, and affirmation phases of instructional delivery supports us in reframing our instructional processes to place the learner at the center of our efforts. BDI strategies, such as U-C-ME, provide learners with a tool in the hand to support their documentation and sharing of background knowledge. Learners then use the tool throughout the remainder of the lesson to scaffold their comprehension, collaboration, talk, and use of new language and concepts. With tangible products to illustrate their learning process, students come to believe that they are capable of academic success, that what they bring to the table matters, and most importantly, that *they* matter.

CHAPTER 3 QUESTIONS FOR REFLECTION AND DISCUSSION

As educators, the first step toward undoing, rethinking, and reimagining is to reflect upon the three C's—challenges, caveats, and considerations—that impact our practices. As professionals in a field that has so many competing agendas, it is critical to reflect upon about our views and perspectives and the role we play in making a difference in the lives of students and families. Reflect on this chapter and independently or collectively with a team, take a position on how you would respond to the following questions.

Challenges

1. How do key stakeholders within the assessment and evaluation process check "habits of doing" to document the assets the learner brings to the teaching and learning context?
2. How will the appropriateness of the assessment and evaluation tools used to gauge linguistic and cognitive development be determined?

Caveats

1. What influence do key stakeholders have on the decision-making processes for identification and placement?
2. How do you adjust to align evaluation and teaching practices with the biopsychosocial history of the learner?

Considerations

1. How will assessment, evaluation, and instruction be monitored to undo the reinforcing cycles of poor educational expectations, experiences, and outcomes for CLD learners?
2. How will the IEP describe the individual child, including unique language assets, accommodations for language supports, and, where feasible, use of the native language?

CHAPTER 4

Enriching Opportunities to Learn Through Collaborative Interaction

Before school even started, I knew Liliana was behind academically. Her intervention log from kindergarten indicated that she struggled with retention of letter names and sounds and had some speech concerns. She was low in all areas, reading, and math, as well as having some focus and behavior concerns. Liliana has definitely come a long way since the beginning of school. She now knows all her letter names and sounds and can recognize and read common 1st-grade spelling patterns.

Being a bilingual teacher, I used that to help her at the beginning—part of the issue was that she did not understand what was being taught or asked of her. Once I noticed she had acquired more English and was talking more in English with me and other students—I began to talk to her more and more in English and less in Spanish. Linking Language [a BDI strategy described in Appendix A] was a great help for Liliana during this time—she started with illustrations, and once she knew her sounds, she added initial sounds and grew from there. It also gave her that much needed talk time with her peers—which I believe was one of the reasons she progressed with her second-language acquisition so quickly.

Now that we are in the last quarter of the school year, Liliana is a much more vocal and confident little girl. We currently use the DOTS chart [a BDI strategy described in Appendix A], and initially she started with more illustrations versus words, but she has begun using more and more words. The tool gives her confidence to share with others both what she already knows and her learning along the way. She is still below grade level, but her gains have been amazing. We had an evaluation for possible SPED [special education], and because of her growth that was not needed!

—Eunice Izazaga, ESOL (English for Speakers of Other Languages) Teacher, 1st Grade

Inclusive classrooms afford teachers and students spaces in which they are able to benefit from the greatest range of human experience. When such contexts are culturally and linguistically diverse, the learning community possesses a wealth of skills, knowledge, lived experiences, beliefs, perspectives, values, symbols, sounds, traditions, household literacies, and community practices that can be leveraged to bring the curriculum to life. Educators such as Ms. Izazaga, who approach teaching and learning from an asset perspective, look for points of entry—doors that will unlock the latent potential that learners possess. In the case of Liliana, this meant searching for the root cause of her current difficulties. As discussed in Chapter 2, utilizing a student's native language is nonnegotiable for determining how the learner is comprehending the intent of the assessment task. Building upon native language skills and encouraging learners to use illustrations to support communication and expression also facilitate English language acquisition and the sharing of knowledge that often goes unobserved by the classroom teacher. All learners have something to share. Our instructional processes must provide learners with the opportunities and scaffolds to facilitate their ability to make their assets public for the learning community.

When approaching lesson delivery, biography-driven instruction (BDI) teachers find ways to maximize the expansive palette of assets that their classroom communities possess by first discovering what each individual brings to the lesson, as discussed in Chapter 3. After activating background knowledge, teachers harness students' words, memories, ideas, and emotions to support connections to the lesson's content and language. Teachers then affirm the learning and language development that has taken place throughout the lesson as students individually demonstrate their conceptual and linguistic understanding. These phases of lesson delivery—activation, connection, affirmation—were introduced in Chapter 3. In this chapter, we turn our attention to ways teachers can use BDI strategies (especially the tool in the hand) to foster joint productive activity and in doing so create an ecology of trust, collaboration, and collective success.

FROM "ME" TO "WE": COMMUNITY PROCESSES AND SHARED PRODUCTS

One of the defining hallmarks of effective pedagogy is the presence of **joint productive activity (JPA)** (Center for Research on Education, Diversity & Excellence [CREDE], 2022). During JPA, the teacher(s) and students work together to *jointly* and collaboratively create products and achieve common goals in the context of meaningful and challenging activities. This type of collaboration, and the conversations that result, support the learning community in developing shared understandings that emerge from the language, skills, and knowledge they bring to the learning space. In culturally and linguistically diverse inclusive classrooms, the question for teachers often becomes, How can I support *all* learners to engage in JPA? From a biography-driven perspective, the answer centers on use of a tool in the hand.

Utilizing a tool in the hand expands students' opportunities to learn by making the socioemotional, linguistic, cognitive, and academic benefits of interaction available for all learners. The tool in the hand serves as both a scaffold and a shared product. There are two aspects of **scaffolding** that are especially pertinent for exceptional learners in CLD classrooms. First, scaffolding provides a conventionalized, ritual *structure* that is both constant and flexible (van Lier, 2004; Walqui & van Lier, 2010). In the case of BDI strategies, learners develop increased comfort with using the hands-on tools when the strategies are implemented on a regular basis. Students are able to use DOTS charts, Vocabulary Quilts, U-C-ME templates, and other graphic organizers (see Appendix A for a brief description of commonly used BDI strategies) to support their learning in increasingly agentic ways. Students come to understand the general purpose of each tool (its "constant" characteristics). They also see how teachers "bend and shape" the tool to meet the needs of the curriculum, and how learners personalize the tool and its use to meet their own needs (its "flexible" characteristics).

A second essential aspect of scaffolding is that it is an interactional *process* that is jointly constructed from moment to moment (van Lier, 2004; Walqui & van Lier, 2010). The process of each strategy provides a recognizable flow, in which the ideas, words, and connections of learners are harvested by the teacher and used to increase the comprehensibility of the lesson's concepts, skills, and language. Students recognize the common expectation that they will use the hands-on tool to document their background knowledge, make connections between the known and the unknown, and use the collection of words and ideas to support their collaborative interactions with peers and their independent work. The hands-on tool becomes more than just a graphic organizer when it is used situationally to facilitate collaborative investigations, discussions, and explorations into how the lesson content is connected to the larger world.

Questions to Consider

How is this view of scaffolding as both a structure and a process similar to your own? How is it different?

Learners continue to build on their strategy tool throughout the lesson. The tool comes to reflect the student's personal ideas, those borrowed from peers, those highlighted by the teacher, and those jointly constructed with other members of the learning community. Because the contributions of the entire class influence what is documented, how the tool is used, and ultimately the finished product, we also refer to BDI strategy tools as "joint products." Given that all learners are working toward development of the joint product, BDI strategies set up the conditions for a natural ebb and flow of interaction that ensures opportunities for communication and collaboration throughout the lesson. When structures that are consistent and flexible are in place to support/scaffold, students enter into learning with the confidence and knowledge that they have the vocabulary and initial conceptual understandings to be able to fully engage without fear of failure. The creation of shared products helps shift the classroom from a more competitive, individualistic environment to a more collectivist ecology centered on the mutual learning and success of all members. Learning, in such ecologies, is experienced as a journey shared by the teacher and learners alike. All members of the classroom community are seen as knowledgeable and capable, and each receives the support needed to progress toward the learning goals.

Based on our (the authors') observations of classrooms across the country, this type of learning ecology stands in stark contrast to the classroom spaces experienced by many CLD learners, especially those with disabilities. Despite the multifaceted benefits of peer interaction, opportunities to engage as full members of the classroom community can be particularly rare for exceptional learners. Students with an IEP frequently are sidelined as they receive individualized support from a special education teacher or paraprofessional who understands their unique needs. Yet without opportunities to sit side-by-side and exchange ideas with their grade-level peers,

exceptional students experience diminished opportunities to learn. A tool in the hand helps level the playing field and allows all learners to engage and benefit from the human resources present in the classroom, rather than having to learn in isolation.

Strategically planning for strategies/tools that will be available to the learner throughout the lesson creates points of entry and access that are not limited by scripted or anticipated responses. BDI strategies foster JPA by explicitly supporting the teacher's use of interactive student groups. Teachers use their knowledge of students' biographies and assets (e.g., background knowledge) to place them in pairs or small groups that will promote their attainment of learning goals. When learners have opportunities to collaborate with one another throughout the lesson, they are able to grow in holistic ways.

MAXIMIZING JOINT PRODUCTIVE ACTIVITY TO RESPOND TO THE WHOLE CHILD

CLD students in inclusive classrooms bring a diverse range of assets, abilities, and individual needs. The curricular goals and learning objectives speak to just one layer of learning and development. Joint productive activity expands the horizon of what can be gained throughout the lesson. In the sections that follow, we highlight how a tool in the hand supports learners in developing along each dimension of their biography (sociocultural, linguistic, cognitive, and academic) as they progress toward attainment of the standards-driven learning goals.

Scaffolding Social Aspects of Learning

Opportunities for peer interaction are vital during core instruction. When students collaborate with their peers, opportunities to practice real-time, face-to-face interpersonal communication naturally occur. Engaging face-to-face sets up the conditions for each participant in the exchange to perceive and appropriately interpret facial expressions, gestures, and other types of body language (Turkle, 2017). When learners have a shared purpose and a common tool in the hand, they have additional context clues to support interpretations of communicative intent and meaning. Students also are more attuned to their peers, because the tool supports them to

Learning in Action Feature 4.1

The products that are developed in the BDI classroom build on the words and ideas of individual learners and the collective group. They reflect instructional conversations and student talk. They incorporate what is independently and jointly written.

share meaningful experiences from their own lives, and this level of personal disclosure fosters natural curiosity about the lives of their classmates. As they generate ideas together, learners draw from their linguistic repertoire, support each other's emotional state, and naturally practice and apply vocabulary related to content learning. This ebb and flow of interaction has the potential to create risk-free spaces where every learner brings a piece of the puzzle. New friendships are forged when life experiences are shared as part of the naturally occurring conversation.

Engaging with others to produce a shared outcome additionally provides opportunities to practice the culturally influenced norms of classroom turn-taking. Such norms can vary significantly from interactional norms in other contexts (e.g., home, soccer field, church). Students who are still developing their understanding of classroom norms benefit from being able to see, and practice alongside, peers engaging with one another. Communication involves back-and-forth sharing of experiences, opinions, and ideas. We use language to engage *with* (not talk at) the people around us. Natural, authentic communication is the goal. An overemphasis on the timing of contributions (e.g., Partner A, then Partner B) can lead to stilted conversations and limited sharing. With a tool in the hand, learners have a scaffold available to support them during the sharing process. Because students are encouraged to use all means of expression available to them (e.g., drawings, symbols, native language, English, gestures), all learners are able to voice their ideas and engage as full members in the exchanges.

Developing conversational social skills is key to learners' successful communication with peers in school settings and also supports their effective communication in nonacademic contexts. Holding conversations with peers who bring different cultural backgrounds, languages, and lived experiences provides opportunities for students to consider alternative perspectives on topics, concepts, processes, and events (Resnick et al., 2010). When students have a tool to document their own ideas as well as various words, images, and ideas borrowed from others, they are able to physically see the broadening of their own perspectives as they learn from one another.

Collaboration fosters interdependence, with each member of the group relying on the others. Interdependence, in turn, increases the social cohesion of the group (Janssen et al., 2010). In other words, if we want to build the type of classroom community where learners encourage and support one another to succeed (All for one and one for all!), we must (1) create opportunities for students to work together to achieve common goals and (2) provide learners with the scaffolds they need to engage meaningfully, equitably, and successfully with their peers.

Learning in Action Feature 4.2

Learners in this 1st-grade classroom use their DOTS charts to support their sharing of background knowledge related to the topic of animals.

Lifting and Leveraging Language

From a linguistic/language development perspective, interaction with peers is an essential source of comprehensible input, especially for CLD students. Through authentic partner and small-group interactions, English learners and exceptional learners have ample opportunities to be givers and receivers of information. As they listen to partners or group members share their perspectives, they are enveloped in words and language structures that frequently are one step beyond what they could produce individually (i+1) (Krashen, 1984/2005). A tool in the hand allows learners to use what is produced independently and collaboratively as building blocks to engage in learning without becoming overwhelmed. Teachers guide all students to record key concepts and essential academic vocabulary words on the tools. Learners also are encouraged to add visuals and words (in any language) that support their individual comprehension and meaning-making processes. Exceptional learners who struggle with language expression and comprehension benefit from opportunities to use multiple means of expression to document their ideas and from having a hands-on tool to reference as they comprehend concepts and language.

When students use tangible tools to document their thoughts and connections, teachers are then able to harvest and lift the language that students produce. Teachers use their knowledge of students' histories and biographies, their awareness of the lesson's learning goals, and their observations of student engagement to make situational decisions about *what* they will highlight, *how* they will do so, and for what purposes. Teachers frequently use the language that students produce to illustrate links to life experiences, exemplify connections to the content, bridge from students' words to the academic vocabulary, make connections between peers' contributions, and support literacy development across languages. When we as teachers model such ways of using tools in the hand to leverage what learners say, write, and think, students become increasingly adept at using strategy tools to support their own learning and language production.

Interacting in partner or small-group settings (as opposed to larger groups) can be considerably less intimidating for learners who are acquiring English. Anxiety surrounding use of the new language is detrimental to comprehension and overall engagement (Krashen, 1982). Within smaller-scale communicative contexts, and with the linguistic support of a tool in the hand, English learners and exceptional learners are more likely to take risks to share ideas and use their developing language skills as they discuss the lesson content. Grouping learners heterogeneously with regard to English proficiency enable peers to serve as language scaffolds for one another, at times playing the role of language model and at other moments serving as the language mentee.

Learning in Action Feature 4.3

Emergent bilingual learners at the middle-school level utilize Foldables and Tri-Folds as they write about and illustrate the processes of evaporation and condensation.

When collaborating with peers who also speak the same native language, emergent bilingual learners have increased opportunities for **translanguaging** (García, 2017), during which they make use of all their linguistic resources to generate ideas and maximize shared knowledge and meaning-making systems. Consider the small-team dialogue captured in the following scenario.

> *Setting the Scene:* A group of four students are variously seated or standing at a table, leaning in to consider the images on the Linking Language poster placed in the middle of the table. Among the students, one learner is identified as gifted, one learner has special needs, and two learners are on/approaching grade level. All the learners are emergent bilinguals who speak English and Spanish. The pictures on the poster reflect different types of land formations. The team members already have individually documented some initial connections to their background knowledge on the poster. Now they are collaborating as a group to discuss what they see and think and record new links. What follows is a snapshot of their conversation.
>
> *Raúl: Cómo se escribe?* [How do you write it?] Uh, what do you guys see?

Pablo: Yo veo [I see] (points to himself), *yo veo agua* [I see water] (points to an image with water).

Raúl: Oh, no, ...

Samuel: It's already there (points to writing on the poster near images that depict water).

Raúl: This is already here (points to the same area of the poster).

Samuel: Ooh! Guys, "This is caused by _____" (points to a sheet with sentence stems laying by the poster). All right. Let's look at this picture (points to an image). I think this is caused by lots of rain flattening the land.

Pablo: (shakes hand with thumb and little finger extended to illustrate agreement)

Samuel: (directed to Emelia) *Escribe que mucho lluvia lo hizo esto* [Write that it was caused because of too much rain] (taps the poster). Ugh (expressing frustration at not knowing the word). How do you say flat *en español* [in Spanish]? (directed to Pablo)

Pablo: Flat?

Samuel: Flat. (passes hand, palm down, over the table to illustrate the idea of flat; looks at Pablo waiting for his answer) Flat, *en español* [in Spanish].

Raúl: Cómo . . . [How].

Pablo: Uh, *cómo* [how], um. (places one palm on top of the other)

Emelia: Negro? [Black?]

Pablo: No.

Raúl: (directed to Emelia) *Qué es esto?* [What is it?] *Qué es esto?* [What is it?] (passes hand, palm down, over the table)

Samuel: (passes hand, palm down, over the table) Flat. *No esto* [Not this] (makes a shape with hands) or *esto* [that] (makes a round shape with hands). *Esto* [This]. (passes hand, palm down, over the table)

Raúl: Flat.

(Team asks someone outside their group for the answer, and the conversation resumes.)

Samuel: Ok, *yo creo que esto es plano porque la lluvia, porque la lluvia lo hace plano* [I think that it is flat because the rain, because the rain makes it flat].

Raúl: (directed to Emelia, who is ready to write) *Pon la lluvia lo hace plano* [Put the rain makes it flat].

Pablo: Acá [Here]. (points to where Emelia should write)

Emelia: (draws line outward from the relevant picture)

Pablo: Uh-huh. *Así, así* [like that, like that].

Teacher: (directed to the team) Tell her how to spell it.

(Team begins to support Emelia to write the idea.)

In this example, the learners draw upon both Spanish and English as they discuss the curricular concepts. The sentence stems provided by the teacher (e.g., "This is caused by _____") serve as additional catalysts for enriching the conversation. The students use whichever language(s) they desire as they share ideas orally. They also use nonverbal language (e.g., hand motions) to communicate their thinking and written language to record their ideas. Throughout the exchange, the communication is natural and the learners support one another in achieving their group goals.

Opportunities to experience translanguaging in the classroom also benefit native English speakers. They are able to hear cognates and different sound

Learning in Action Feature 4.4

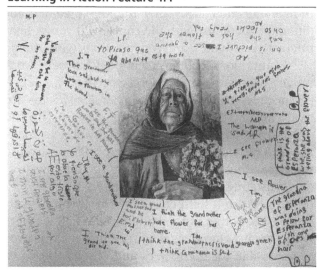

This Linking Language poster illustrates the power of allowing emergent bilinguals to utilize all their language resources as they make connections to background knowledge.

systems, learn words in new languages, and see the excited engagement of their peers, which frequently accompanies communication that occurs in the home language. **Metalinguistic awareness** for all learners is bolstered through classroom interactions in which language differences and similarities are viewed as additional launch points for conversation, connections to background knowledge, and avenues for exploring the content (Escamilla et al., 2013; Herrera, 2022).

Catalyzing Cognition

From a cognitive perspective, we cannot know in advance exactly how learners will make sense of the curriculum. How many times have we experienced students making myriad connections and quickly comprehending a concept after a brief discussion with classmates, while our own meticulously planned explanation resulted in more than one blank stare? As students listen to peers' ideas, they seek clarification of thoughts from one another as well as rationales for viewpoints and conclusions. These types of exchanges challenge all learners to increased levels of cognitive rigor. They can yield better decision-making and bolster creative thinking (Johnson & Johnson, 1979, 2007). A tool in the hand supports such processes by allowing students to organize their thinking and frequently revisit and re-evaluate their ideas after they have gained additional experience with the concepts through text, interactive activities, and conversations with others.

Assumptions about exceptional learners' cognitive processes—and more specifically, deficit perspectives connected to *assumed limitations*—are easily made when we provide all learners with the same input, expect a uniform process of sensemaking, and provide a single avenue for demonstrating understanding and learning. Such assumptions lead to devastating cumulative effects on the learning trajectories and self-perceptions of learners with disabilities. A tool in the hand provides all learners with a means of making their meaning-making processes visible for themselves and others. It further helps students manage the cognitive load of classroom activities.

Dialogic exchanges, typically geared toward eliciting higher order thinking (Sedova et al., 2014), can generate an increased cognitive load, especially for emergent bilingual and exceptional learners. Learners are required to use memory to "hold" comments shared by peers as they wait for appropriate opportunities to respond. At the same time, they are planning their own contributions to the initial prompt, activity, or question posed. The rapid pace at which varying perspectives and ideas are shared can make conversational interactions particularly challenging. As Gu and Cai (2019) note, group coordination (e.g., exchange of ideas, interaction, communication) comes at a cognitive cost (termed "transaction cost").

A tool in the hand can help anchor the learner's thought process and alleviate the cognitive pressure that might otherwise silence or immobilize the learner. Students are able to allocate fewer cognitive resources to holding information because the tool allows them to make notes, draw arrows, link ideas, and use the tool in any way that supports their meaningful engagement with the content and language of the lesson. Learners then are at greater liberty to apply their cognitive resources toward engaging in communicative exchanges, exercising their critical thinking skills, and applying their creative capacities (Chick, 2014; Gu & Cai, 2019).

The shared nature of collaborative tasks during JPA provides the additional benefit of reducing the task-related cognitive load, since it is distributed among group members (Janssen et al., 2010). A task that would be overwhelming if encountered individually becomes more manageable when approached with the support, camaraderie, and synergy of a team, with each member contributing their knowledge, skills, perspectives, and experiences. Opportunities to interact with peers thus provide all learners the ongoing cognitive advantage of being stretched to engage in their zone of proximal development (ZPD) (Vygotsky, 1978). Rather than being a static zone of optimal learning, the ZPD shifts as learners develop new conceptual insights and gain prowess with curricular skills and language.

Questions to Consider

In what ways do you provide regular, purposeful opportunities for exceptional CLD learners to collaborate with peers in small groups? What tool in the hand do learners have for scaffolding and documenting their cognitive processes?

Learning in Action Feature 4.5

Learners in this 4th-grade classroom collaborate in small groups to discuss westward expansion. The Vocabulary Quilt serves as a tool in the hand to support their connections to the grade-level concepts and language. It also provides a concrete scaffold for student-led conversations that challenge all members to think more deeply about the content.

Teachers likewise use what is captured on the learning tools, such as learners' links to background knowledge, connections between concepts, and visuals/ideas related to the vocabulary, to gauge how students are cognitively processing the new material. What learners record on the tool in the hand provides entry points to one-on-one conversations, strategic questioning, and opportunities for students to articulate their thinking. Joint productive activity in a BDI classroom community is not limited to small-group contexts, as conceptualized by some researchers (Mellom et al., 2019), but also is maximized within the context of the whole group. Teachers use the insights they gather as they circulate among pairs and small teams to situationally decide how students' thinking can be used to advance the learning of the entire classroom community. Anchor charts and BDI tools that are projected or displayed allow the teacher to revoice key connections and model the linking of ideas for the whole group.

Voices From the Field

In the beginning of the year, this sharing and making of connections in conversations looks more like me facilitating discussions and asking questions to prompt the sharing of additional information. However, as the year progresses, the students naturally know how to make meaningful connections to the lesson's topic, concept, or skill. These norms consider emotional safety regarding student participation in order to keep students' affective filters lowered, but I also must consider student biographies throughout active lessons in order to ensure my students can participate effectively in the lesson and attain the "+1" knowledge from the lesson.

—Kelsey Erickson, Elementary ELL Teacher

Accelerating Academic Achievement

Academic gains result when learners have consistent opportunities for purposeful, scaffolded interaction. Research indicates that discussion and collaboration (i.e., seeking help from peers) are among the most effective practices to promote consolidation of deep learning (Hattie & Donoghue, 2016). Positive goal interdependence, which occurs in the context of JPA, fosters both productivity and achievement (Johnson & Johnson, 2009). Students increase their efforts to succeed when they know their contributions will influence the learning outcomes of others.

This interconnectedness and feeling of being an integral member of the learning community are missing for many exceptional learners. A tool in the hand, therefore, allows all learners to be equal members of the learning community. With the support that the tool offers, they are able to share their thinking, build upon the contributions of others, and advance linguistically and conceptually. Exceptional students experience an increased sense of belonging when they are valued for who they are *and* for what they contribute to the learning process. As they collaborate with their peers, learners have opportunities to articulate their understanding, summarize information, and elaborate on ideas, all of which have long been shown to support the retention of learning and academic

Figure 4.1. Benefits of Scaffolded Learning Across Classroom Contexts

Inclusive, Grade-Level Classrooms	• Students receiving core instruction are supported to participate as full members of the learning community. • Students being monitored as part of PSPs are able to utilize their full range of assets (sociocultural, linguistic, cognitive, academic) to engage in and demonstrate learning.
Pullout Classrooms	• Students receiving Tier 2 interventions benefit from tools that provide additional context for skill development tasks. • Students have tools to support their use of language with peers in partner and small-group activities.
Self-Contained Classrooms	• Students have hands-on tools that make learning more concrete and less abstract. • Students' tools provide teachers the flexibility to differentiate tasks according to their individual learning goals.

achievement (Johnson & Johnson, 1991; Johnson et al., 1985). As illustrated in Figure 4.1, CLD learners in all types of classroom contexts benefit from scaffolded engagement opportunities.

FOSTERING JOINT PRODUCTIVE ACTIVITY THROUGH i+TpsI

Students gain the most when they are able to reap the benefits of both individual and social aspects of learning. The mnemonic "**i+TpsI**" (pronounced "I tipsy" and explained in this chapter) supports teachers to consider the types of interactions and grouping structures used throughout the lesson. The typical flow of instruction in U.S. classrooms is marked by direct instruction, student practice, and individual accountability (I do, we do, you do). By contrast, BDI teachers begin by inviting the individual learner (represented with "i") into the lesson. This little "i" reflects the uncertainty that learners often feel as they begin a new topic or unit of study. An unspoken question lingering in the minds of many students is, Does what I know matter? As discussed in Chapter 3, teachers implementing BDI make clear that what learners already know (e.g., funds of knowledge, prior knowledge, academic knowledge) not only matters but is *fundamental* to the entire lesson. The learning process, therefore, is initiated by activating background knowledge. The flow of BDI instruction, in its simplest form, reflects *you do*, I do, we do, you do.

After students use a tool in the hand to make their background knowledge public for the teacher and

their peers, the teacher engages learners in teacher-directed, text-driven, total-group interactions (T). Students gain insights into new vocabulary and begin to grapple with the curricular concepts. The capital "T" locates the power with the teacher, given that the teacher is the one in control and responsible for supporting learners to comprehend and make meaning. As learning progresses, the teacher intersperses regular opportunities for students to interact with pairs/partners (p) and in small teams (s). Pairs/partners frequently are used to allow students to check their understanding by sharing ideas, comparing answers, clarifying through the native language, or making additional connections to lived experiences. Small teams, on the other hand, commonly support perspective taking, consensus building, and students' facilitation of learning for one another.

As students collaborate and discuss ideas with classmates, the teacher circulates to provide support, prompt deeper thinking, and elicit rationales for ideas that students share orally or through illustrations or in writing. Rather than merely monitoring students for on-task behavior, the teacher observes how learners are making sense of the new information. The formative assessment information that is gathered helps the teacher determine the following:

- When to pull the group back together for whole-group conversation
- How to "tell a story" that pulls all the works/voices/knowledge of the community into a cohesive discussion of the content where everyone's contribution is valued
- When to provide additional direct instruction

- What kinds of additional scaffolding and modeling might be needed
- What individual and group gains should be affirmed
- What adjustments and next steps might further the learning of the class

Although some opportunities for peer interaction are preplanned and likely to appear in the teacher's lesson plan, many are determined situationally, based on how students are responding in the moment (see Chapter 3 for discussion of contextual and situational processes).

When making decisions about which particular students to partner or place in each group, teachers consider factors such as these:

- Learners' biopsychosocial histories and biographies
- Learners' individualized learning goals
- The purpose of the specific interaction (e.g., developing socioemotional skills, exploring an issue from multiple perspectives, developing listening and speaking skills, comprehending the text, practicing and applying new processes)
- Pre-assessment information gained in the activation phase
- Learners' current socioemotional states of mind
- Time available for the peer interaction

Knowing our classroom community and developing our capacities to "read" the situation allows us to make increasingly effective grouping decisions that keep all learners moving productively toward the goal.

By the end of the lesson, students have had multiple opportunities to interact with the targeted concepts and language of the lesson, and they have benefited from the scaffolding provided by peers, personalized learning tools, and curricular resources. They are confident and prepared to demonstrate what they know on tasks that allow for individual accountability (I). The capital "I" reflects the individual learner who has been empowered, through their successes with learning, language, and social interaction, to see themselves as increasingly capable members of the classroom community. Figure 4.2 provides a checklist to support self-assessment and reflection on the ways i+TpsI grouping

configurations are used to maximize students' assets and support development of each dimension of the learner's biography throughout the lesson.

USING BDI STRATEGIES TO GUIDE INTERACTIONAL PROCESSES

Teachers who use BDI strategies engage with learners in ways that reflect higher levels of JPA (MacDonald et al., 2013; Pérez et al., 2012). Why is this? Simply put, BDI strategies are purposefully designed to support a reciprocal interplay between the teacher and student, and between the student and peers, throughout the lesson. As previously discussed, BDI strategies include tools that scaffold students' participation in social exchanges, cognitive processing, and language production. These tools also serve as a common product that is developed throughout the course of instruction. Sometimes students work collaboratively to add to a shared tool (e.g., Linking Language poster). At other times, they have their own individual tool. The end result is that *everyone* is working toward the same overarching goals and using the same type of tool to support them along the way (joint product).

In inclusive classrooms, BDI strategies provide teachers with the flexibility to differentiate for each learner's needs and provide varying degrees of cognitive and linguistic challenge. The subsequent sections offer a close-up look at the DOTS (Determine, Observe, Talk, Summarize) BDI strategy, with a special focus on how grouping configurations and student interaction factor into each phase of the lesson.

From A to Z: Multiple Points of Entry

BDI strategies allow all learners to enter the lesson from their own starting point. The "D" in DOTS stands for *Determine*. Using the alpha boxes on the DOTS chart, learners are provided with an open "canvas of opportunity." They have the freedom to use pictures and words to document what they already know about the topic, which is written at the top of the chart. Teachers approach the beginning of the lesson from the perspective of discovering assets and building background rather than identifying weaknesses and filling gaps. What students *do* know and *can* do are pivotal to an effective, culturally and

Figure 4.2. i+Tpsl Grouping Configurations Checklist

Grouping	What did you do to support your CLD students' sociocultural, linguistic, academic, and cognitive dimensions throughout the learning process?
i = Individual student	☐ Student interest in the lesson was sparked through stimulation of one or more of the five senses. ☐ All students were provided with opportunities to document and share their initial connections between the topic and their background knowledge (i.e., funds of knowledge, prior knowledge, and academic knowledge). ☐ Awareness and understanding of learners' biopsychosocial histories informed responses to the ideas and language produced.
T = Teacher-directed, text-driven, total group	☐ Whole-group modeling, discussion, and/or authentic application of learnings in practice occurred. ☐ Whole-group activities were structured to provide explicit opportunities for CLD students to interact with their peers. ☐ Students were provided with opportunities to discuss, synthesize, and infer from their own unique perspectives as they participated in group discussions. ☐ Whole-group activities were strategically designed to provide emergent bilinguals with English language modeling by the teacher and/or more proficient peers as they interacted to enhance their understanding of the text and concepts.
p = Pairs/partners	☐ CLD students worked with partners to support their comprehension of academic tasks through one-on-one discussion and authentic practice and application of content-based learnings. ☐ Emergent bilinguals worked with a more proficient peer who could speak the native language and clarify information in the native language, if needed. ☐ Partners produced a product that demonstrated their understanding of a critical concept or vocabulary term.
s = Small teams	☐ Students worked in small teams so that they could hear multiple perspectives, check their understanding, build consensus, and elaborate on their own schemas. ☐ Teams were purposely configured so that emergent bilinguals were able to see and hear language modeled by more proficient peers. ☐ Small teams were held accountable to demonstrate their learnings informally or formally.
I = Individual accountability	☐ Students independently practiced and applied their learnings. ☐ Individual activities allowed students to demonstrate what they had learned. ☐ Authentic assessments were implemented that enabled emergent bilinguals at multiple language proficiency levels to successfully demonstrate their learnings.

Source: Herrera, Socorro G., *Biography-Driven Culturally Responsive Teaching*, 3rd Ed., © 2022, Figure 8.7, p. 127. Reprinted by permission of Teachers College Press, New York, New York.

linguistically responsive lesson. Figure 4.3 provides a DOTS chart related to the topic of real numbers.

After students have individually added to their charts, they often have an opportunity to compare ideas with a partner. Perhaps they agree with what their classmate shared. Maybe the conversation sparks additional memories, images, words, and ideas. In BDI classrooms, the emphasis is on building together, not competing with one another. Students are encouraged to borrow words and ideas and add them to their own charts, often circling or

notating in some fashion which words were gained through interactions with a friend. The teacher explains that they will continue adding words to their DOTS charts throughout the lesson.

As the teacher begins to bridge into the content, learners are guided to add the target vocabulary words around the margins of the chart. They then have a brief opportunity to make initial connections between the outside words (the vocabulary) and the inside words (their background knowledge). Initial connections are typically made with pencil,

Figure 4.3. Determining the Known

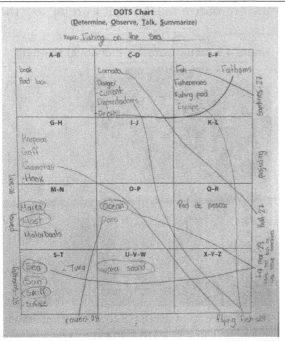

A newcomer student at the middle-school level used this DOTS chart to activate and record connections to mathematical knowledge that had been accumulated from experiences in the home, community, and school.

since the class has yet to dive into the text and begin learning about the words. These connections, however, provide the teacher with a glimpse into what learners already know about the vocabulary. Again, a quick opportunity to share with a partner allows learners to hear additional perspectives and receive affirmation from peers for their own ideas.

Connecting the Dots

The "O" in DOTS stands for *Observe*. As the teacher leads the class through an exploration of the content using the text and other curricular resources (e.g., media, visuals), students are encouraged to observe and make connections to what they are learning. They add new words to the alpha boxes and record the meanings of the vocabulary terms as they are encountered in text, often noting the corresponding page number beside the term and using the reverse side or a separate piece of paper to jot notes about each word's meaning. They draw lines to connect the vocabulary with the images and words inside the chart, which now reflect the learner's background knowledge as well as other words relevant to the topic.

The DOTS chart in Figure 4.4 illustrates the types of connections made by an emergent bilingual high

Figure 4.4. Observing for New Understandings

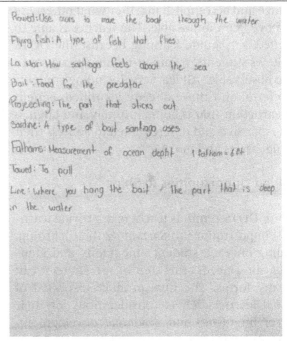

This DOTS chart illustrates how one high school learner linked the academic vocabulary words (located around the boxes) to the other words and ideas on the chart and defined the words throughout the lesson.

school learner as she connected words from her background knowledge to the academic vocabulary used in *The Old Man and the Sea*. Page numbers frequently were included to support her ability to reference the book. As the class encountered each vocabulary word in the text, the student recorded the definition in relation to the topic of fishing on the sea.

The "T" of DOTS reminds teachers and students that *Talk* is essential for meaning making. Teachers provide opportunities for students to discuss their learning, connections, and new ideas in small groups of four or five. Students can ask questions to clarify their understanding of the vocabulary. They also can see how their peers are connecting the academic vocabulary to their own words and lives beyond the classroom. The teacher circulates to spend time with each group, listening, engaging in the conversation, and scanning to see the connections that students are recording. Knowledge of the learning community informs the teacher's decisions about which groups or particular students might need to be visited first to provide additional support. Observations about what is being produced also make clear which groups and learners might need extra attention.

Through i+TpsI, the community jointly elevates the potential of each learner. The DOTS chart serves as the tool in the hand, scaffolding learners to produce and accomplish together what otherwise would have been impossible. The teacher is able to more effectively guide learning because the DOTS chart allows students' meaning-making processes to become observable. All learners, including students in prereferral and those already identified, benefit from instruction that is both culturally and linguistically responsive and differentiated to address their individual assets and needs.

Scaffolded Opportunities to Shine

The "S" in DOTS reminds teachers to provide learners with opportunities to *Summarize* their learning. Depending on each student's biography and identified learning needs, this step of the strategy can take many forms. The final products expected of individual learners reflect considerations for their cognitive, linguistic, and academic development. Teachers can easily provide individual accommodations to ensure each learner has the support

needed to succeed. For English learners new to the language, this might involve collaborating with a home-language peer to discuss what was learned and then drawing an image to illustrate key ideas. For some students a written summary would be appropriate. In all cases, students have their individual DOTS chart (and often the class version as well) to support their completion of the postinstructional task. They have a personalized word bank to draw from in addition to the connections they have discussed and physically represented on their charts.

Students often have opportunities to share their summaries in some fashion with their peers. Depending on the learners, this might mean sharing with a single partner or with their small-team members. The teacher might ask for volunteers to read their summaries aloud for the class, or ask each student to share one of their favorite sentences, images, or ideas. What matters is finding ways to celebrate the learning and accomplishments evident within the classroom community. Because students began at their own starting points, their finish lines will also differ, yet each will have made progress toward achieving the shared learning goals. Their personalized learning tools provide evidence of the growth and learning gains they have made. Figure 4.5 illustrates how the DOTS chart serves as a scaffold throughout the lesson as students use their resources to take their learning to writing.

Figure 4.5. Demonstrating Individual Learning

This student used his DOTS chart, in combination with other curricular resources, to express his understanding of genre and point of view.

CONCLUSION

What we can accomplish by working together is infinitely greater than what any single individual can accomplish on their own. This chapter illustrated how a tool in the hand provides the scaffolding—as both a structure and a process—to ensure that each student is able to engage in shared learning processes with their peers. It also explored how teachers can work in collaboration with learners to create joint products that testify to the conceptual and linguistic advances that are possible for *all learners* when interaction is maximized in inclusive classrooms. The i+TpsI mnemonic was provided as a

means for checking habits of practice to ensure that every lesson begins with the assets of the individual learner, incorporates high-quality whole-group instruction, and affords multiple opportunities for learners to engage in authentic communication with peers in pairs and small teams. Learners arrive at the end of BDI lessons prepared to demonstrate their advances in understanding and ability in ways that foster individual accountability. The chapter concluded with a close-up look at the DOTS strategy, which illustrated how the processes and tools of BDI strategies support all learners to contribute to the learning community, benefit from JPA, and maximize their individual potential.

CHAPTER 4 QUESTIONS FOR REFLECTION AND DISCUSSION

As educators, the first step toward undoing, rethinking, and reimagining is to reflect upon the three C's—challenges, caveats, and considerations—that impact our practices. As professionals in a field that has so many competing agendas, it is critical to reflect upon about our views and perspectives and the role we play in making a difference in the lives of students and families. Reflect on this chapter and independently or collectively with a team, take a position on how you would respond to the following questions.

Challenges

1. How does the prescriptive curriculum impact core instruction and interventions used for ensuring access for the learner?
2. How does the ecology of classroom allow for joint productive activity given the daily pacing of instruction?

Caveats

1. In what ways does the sociopolitical context of your classroom support or deny use of the native language and the cultural assets of the learner and their family?
2. How do you adjust to align practices to the realities of students and their families?

Considerations

1. How will the ecology of the classroom be orchestrated to maximize access to the general education curriculum for all learners?
2. In what ways might scaffolding, as both a structure and a process, be maximized in new ways to enhance students' opportunities to learn?

CHAPTER 5

Creating Contexts and Conditions for an Inclusive Community Through Classroom Talk

Alejandro [pseudonym] came to me as an extremely low student. I met with the child study team by the second day of school to inquire about his extremely low academics. His reading and writing skills were at a kindergarten level when he was tested. Previous years noted his attendance issues. His mom mentioned that he cried a lot and didn't want to go to school so she would let him stay home. School was not an enjoyable place for Alejandro. Throughout the year I noticed significant changes. His attendance started greatly improving and his interactions with myself and his peers started improving. I believe using the BDI strategies in the classroom is the reason for these improvements. At the beginning of the year he was barely able to complete one full sentence. By the end of the year, he was able to write five to seven sentences on topic. His participation in class discussions improved because BDI strategies and tools gave him the ability to retain information that he previously struggled with. At conferences his mom shed tears at the amount of improvement she has seen in him this year, not only in academics, but also in not fighting her to come to school every morning. I believe using BDI in the classroom helped Alejandro to feel successful academically and socially.

—Victoria Clark, 4th-Grade Teacher

In the vignette above, the teacher acknowledges that Alejandro was not on grade level when he arrived in her classroom. Often, learners bring with them the accumulated effects of schooling experiences that have left them doubting their own capacities based on labels, low expectations grounded within a history reflecting a deficit perspective on culture, language, and ways of knowing. As discussed in Chapter 3, the ways in which systems have responded to the biopsychosocial history of the learner often dictate what the learning ecology feels like for the CLD learner in the classroom. When learning spaces do not feel safe and affirming, CLD students may feel excluded during instruction (Hammond, 2015), often taking on self-defensive coping strategies that can take the form of acting out behaviorally, refusing to engage in activities, remaining silent in classroom discussions, reducing their visibility (e.g., pulling a hoodie over their face, slumping on their desk to bury their head in their arms), or being entirely absent from school. Students also may avoid taking ownership over their learning and instead may become overly dependent on adults for participating in whole-group, partner, or small-team activities.

As explored in Chapter 3, learning about and understanding the biopsychosocial history of learners is pivotal to making sense of where they are psychologically and emotionally and understanding why they may react to instruction in nonresponsive ways. Every learner needs to feel capable of success and perceive that the conditions in the classroom are such that regardless of cultural background, language, or disability they are contributing members of the learning community. Contributions may be expressed in multiple forms and, when learning becomes a collective versus individual act, every learner has the opportunity to engage in and contribute to the learning goal. For many learners in the response to intervention process or referral process and for exceptional learners, their limitations/disabilities—rather than their abilities—have been the focus. This skewed focus reinforces a deficit perspective that can quickly become self-fulfilling for learners. Teachers hold the power to create classroom conditions that provide opportunities for all learners to be active and engaged participants who make contributions springing from who they are and what they know and then use those assets as building blocks for current learning.

In Chapter 4, we illustrated how BDI strategies can be used to integrate and scaffold opportunities for interaction. We highlighted how joint productive activity (with a tool in the hand) provides students with a common goal and how it involves teacher(s) and students collaborating to move learning forward. Yet how exactly does one orchestrate teaching and learning to achieve the lesson goals and simultaneously ensure learners are reaching their individual social and academic potentials? How do we make sure students are contributing to the learning community throughout the lesson? What key factors are necessary for joint productive activity to come to life in word and action? What role does the CLD student biography (sociocultural, linguistic, cognitive, and academic) play during instruction? Chapter 5 explores questions such as these through the lens of instructional conversation. It takes a close-up look at the processes, tools, and language practices that teachers can use to ensure all students have equitable opportunities to engage as equal members of the learning community.

CATALYZING LEARNING THROUGH COMMUNITY: CARING AND LEARNING IN ACTION

Learning is first and foremost about authentic relationships—relationships that acknowledge, accept, respect, and allow both people to draw from each other, while also recognizing and working around our limitations. Community as an ecology is first a gut feeling where learners perceive they are either accepted and supported or labeled and excluded. Context determines what is possible, and teacher actions that set conditions for building community begin from the moment learners enter the classroom. Learners quickly notice how their "uniqueness" is not labeled or highlighted through exclusion; instead, they see inclusion reflected and made possible by the orchestration of space, materials, and interactions that lay the foundation for acceptance/understanding.

Voices From the Field

One way to gauge a CLD student's general knowledge, skills, and experiences upon arrival in class is to have students to fill out a biography card (see example in Figure 5.1). Students' biographies inform us, enlighten us, and challenge us in our planning, so it is essential to understand the funds of knowledge our students bring with themselves to the classroom, such as where they are from, what languages they speak, what goals they have, and how they feel about school. By understanding their background knowledge and experiences, we can further enrich their learning, aid them in making connections to academic content, and make their learning relevant. By knowing students' biographies, we are challenged as educators to use that knowledge to find ways to represent and link to their cultures and traditions in ways that speak to each of our students. When we know more about our students, we can make informed decisions about best practices and use the students as resources in their own classroom learning.

—Stephanie Loganbill, High School
(Algebra 1 and Geometry Essentials)

Students observe each word, action, and interaction, gathering information as they "test the winds" in the new learning space. The teacher's routines, expectations, and use of language set the stage for student engagement, language production, critical thinking, and collaboration. Learners make decisions about questions such as, Is it safe to share my real self? Does what I know matter? How do I fit into this group? Is it all right to make mistakes? Will I have to figure everything out on my own? What does the teacher think about me? How do my peers view me?

Learning requires risk taking. Building trust is embodied in the way we as educators work with the flow of conversation. Often we are focused on learning outcomes, academic talk, and pacing/time; within the scope of how the day is structured, the sociocultural dimension is lost in transition from one task to the next. Authentic instructional conversations are first and foremost framed and guided by the learner's personal experiences, identity, assets,

Figure 5.1. Sample CLD Student Biography Card

Student Information	L1 Proficiency: Spanish	L2 Proficiency: English	Prior Schooling	Academic/Assessment
Name: VM Age: 17 Grade: 11 Born: Uruguay Time in USA: 3 years	Oral: Advanced Writing: Advanced Reading: Intermediate Based on: _X_ Observation ___ Test ___ Both	Oral: Beginning Writing: Intermediate Reading: Intermediate Based on: _X_ Observation ___ Test ___ Both SLA: Intermediate Fluency	Lived in Uruguay for 6 years, Venezuela for 8 years, Florida for 1 year, and has lived in Kansas for 2 years. <hr>**Parental Support** Parent does not know English and does not help with math, but is a Spanish-speaking psychologist.	Solves math problems on paper. Can work independently or with a partner/small group. Does well at initiating questions when she has them. She does not like to speak in front of the whole group but does fine when I work with her in her small group or one-on-one.

Source: Stephanie Loganbill, High School (Algebra 1 and Geometry Essentials)

and challenges. Accessing and elaborating upon students' richly networked schemas hold the greatest potential for their learning and retention. Yet without regular authentic exchanges of ideas, trust, along with the connections that students make and the responses they provide (if they provide any at all), will remain superficial.

Context is about the "i," as discussed in Chapter 3. How and where we position ourselves, the community, and most importantly the learner determine the quality and depth of conversation or dialogue. Creating a culturally and linguistically responsive context requires us as educators to listen and learn, harvest the details of our learners' experiences, explore how they use language to share ideas, and use their words and ideas to bridge into the content. Context matters in ways we are not always attuned to during instruction. How often in setting the conditions for talk to occur are we so focused on the sentence stems that will be used that we forget which grouping configurations will best leverage the assets of each contributor in the community? How will we observe the learner's response? What lifts or silences the learner's voice? What language is used to communicate? How is the student transferring knowledge from one language to the other? What are the learning challenges students are facing in the classroom? Why are these questions so important when a CLD learner is in the referral process or receiving services?

From our perspective as researchers and educators, the typical context and curriculum have the potential of classrooms remaining bound by the perspective of the teacher, the curriculum publisher, and the historically monocultural and monolingual educational system. By contrast, **instructional conversations** that foster trust, maximize the diversity of learners present, and nurture a culturally and linguistically responsive ecology have at least three things in common: (1) they center the learner, (2) they involve a reciprocal ebb and flow of communication, and (3) they reflect equitable patterns of interaction.

BEGINNING WITH BIOGRAPHIES: EQUITY BEGINS WITH "i"

As educators, we philosophically agree that our planning for instruction is fundamentally grounded in actions to meet learners at their "point of departure." However, in practice, achieving this in real time within diverse classrooms can become a daunting task. Our educator's mindset (depending on the decade in which our teacher preparation took place) has conditioned many of us to prepare the learner for the "measurable" learning objective. By asking students to respond to a "please do now" prompt on the board or using an anticipatory set, a pretest, or another prelesson activity, we attempt to gather information about the knowledge and skills that learners possess. Yet these opportunities are often abstract and disconnected from the learner's background knowledge, and the resulting output provides few insights into learners' lives and what they know about the vocabulary, topic, or content to be taught. Often our educator's mindset stays within the IEP box, colored by our assumptions regarding the limited experiences, knowledge, or language abilities of the learner. After all (our thinking goes), the reason the student is being referred or receives services is related to their performance on grade-level tasks and/or language differences.

At the core, equity in learning is fundamentally about providing a risk-free opportunity for the interpretation and sharing of experience and knowledge that a learner possesses. It is in this magical moment of allowing thought to occur that learning pathways are opened for inclusion that allows for multiple representations of knowledge, use of the native language(s), and personal expression. Think about the following scenario:

> As I sat in the back of the room and observed as Mr. George (pseudonym) initiated the Linking Language strategy as part of the beginning of a unit on habitats, I noted a boy sitting in the middle of the room with an iPad. The class was preparing to work, first with partners to initiate a quick write on what they knew about the word *habitat*, and then in small teams to circulate around the room and respond to pictures of animals the teacher had laid out for activating background knowledge (as discussed in Chapter 3). Mr. George read out the names of partners and had listed the names for teams on the board. I noticed that the boy's name was neither called nor listed. I walked over to Mr. George and asked why the boy was excluded. His response was that the child was not very social and his IEP stated that he preferred to work on the iPad. I asked why he was not on the same topic, and Mr. George's response was that the student usually did his own thing. I then asked Mr. George if he would allow me to talk to this young man about how he might contribute to the activity. He agreed, although he reiterated that the learner preferred to work alone.
>
> I approached Shawn (pseudonym) with the visuals that all the other students were using, and I asked him to pick his favorite animal and use his iPad to find as many pictures as possible that would help me understand where that animal lived. I followed up

with him every few minutes as the other students rotated around the room writing or drawing in response to the pictures (see Linking Language, Appendix A). I then asked him to move to the next animal pictured. As the task was completed and the students all returned to whole-class instruction to explore the habitats of different animals, I asked the teacher to borrow Shawn's iPad and display it on the document camera as he shared out what the class had concluded about each of the animals. The teacher's goal was to integrate some of the pictures as he described what he had learned from what the teams had produced. It was important to point out how Shawn had contributed to the community by aligning his pictures with the words and findings of the community. In this way, an equitable space was created, drawing upon Shawn's technology skills as he connected to the content. As the lesson moved into text and writing later in the week, the community used the pictures, which Mr. George had printed out, to enhance what had been written independently by each member of the class.

In this classroom, Shawn had many ideas to share with his peers. Providing equitable opportunities for participation meant finding ways to leverage his assets toward his expression of connections to the content (e.g., pictures of the animals' habitats). Such maximization of each learner's knowledge, skills, and ideas requires purposeful planning. Core instruction during the prereferral and referral phases must set conditions that allow for the learner to express and produce from a place that is respectful and trusting and that allows for strengths to break past traditional ways of doing.

Context often defines the boundaries of what is possible for the community.

An effective, inclusive ecology utilizes learners' strengths with an awareness of challenges/limitations, configuring the community in ways that allow every interaction to be characterized by lifting one another and expressing authentic *cariño* (caring respect) in addressing the challenges. In Chapters 3 and 4, we illustrated how BDI strategies offer opportunities for all learners to document connections to their background knowledge. However, using strategy tools is only one piece of the puzzle. Our words and nonverbal communication also are key to students' willingness to invest in the activation process and make their ideas public.

Consider the following excerpt of an instructional conversation that took place during the activation phase of a 1st-grade lesson (Holmes, 2022). As you read, identify the teacher's words and behaviors that created an inviting, welcoming, and risk-free opportunity for students to share with the freedom and flexibility to enter into learning with whatever words, knowledge, and skills they had available.

Teacher: I'm going to show you what our posters are for this week. (Teacher holds up Linking Language posters for the class to see, as they sit on the carpet.) Now, this week, our theme is going to be the arts. And our focus will be music. So thinking (points to her head) about that and thinking about these posters (points to the middle of the poster facing the students), you guys are going to go through and write what it reminds you of (points to her head), what it makes you think about (holds hand out, palm up), or how (places hand over heart) it makes you feel. And so take a look at these two photographs that I have today. This is the first one (shows picture of a heartbeat image, like what might be found on a heart monitor). And this is the other one (shows picture of a man riding a unicycle). [. . .] You guys will take turns writing what it makes you think about, reminds you about, or how it makes you feel. You have your Linking Language markers with you. Listen (points to head) carefully so you know which poster you will be going to this morning first. (The teacher begins to place students in small groups.) Remember, we can write or we can draw. (Teacher begins to circulate among groups.) What do you see, what does it remind you of, what does it make you think about, or how does it make you feel?

(The teacher approaches a small group.)

Teacher: Maricela, what are you drawing? (approaches and crouches down beside student)

Maricela: A doctor.

Teacher: A doctor. And why are you drawing a doctor?

Maricela: Because doctors have this (references the image of the heartbeat) to make people, um, feel better. (looks up at teacher)

Teacher: Oh, so you've (points to picture) seen that (Maricela nods) in a doctor's office where they make people feel better? (gestures toward the poster) Okay. (Maricela begins to write on the poster)

Luis (another member of the small group): Um, doctors freak me out . . . and I got a band-aid over that.

Teacher: (speaking to Luis) So if that scares you, what can you draw on your Linking Language poster?

In this scenario, the teacher provided learners with multiple points of entry. She reiterated numerous ways that students might connect to the images on the Linking Language posters (e.g., "What do you see, what does it remind you of, what does it make you think about, or how does it make you feel?") She used hand gestures to support learners' comprehension of the task. She also reminded learners they could write or draw. The teacher actively observed students as they documented ideas on their tool in the hand and then stopped to have direct exchanges with learners about what they were drawing and writing. These interactions provided her with insights into their lives (e.g., experiences in the community), biographies (e.g., oral language and literacy skills), and biopsychosocial histories (e.g., emotional memories). Such information gathered at the beginning of the lesson is then available to fuel ongoing conversations, build connections between learners, and make connections to the content that are meaningfully linked to learners. This harvesting of words and ideas takes little time. It simply requires that the teacher be intentionally present to learners and attend to what they are producing.

Context matters when we plan for instructional conversations and affirming students' languages and cultural backgrounds. Knowing who is in the room and their assets and challenges is critical for orchestrating talk that is equitable. Intentionally planning for talk means fostering authentic exchanges not derived from a textbook with prefabricated questions, but from the dynamic way in which the textbook has been brought to life for all learners in the classroom.

Learning in Action Feature 5.1

The 1st-grade teacher observes to see what this small team of learners is recording on the Linking Language poster. She asks questions to elicit student talk, as they use words to label and explain their connections to background knowledge.

Questions to Consider

In what ways do you harvest words and ideas from your classroom community? How do you use what the community produces to think about the context and set the conditions to draw on strengths (deepen knowledge) and plan targeted challenges, using social-affective strategies (people/talk) to scaffold community learning?

SITUATIONALLY SPEAKING: THE EBB AND FLOW OF RECIPROCAL TALK

An essential characteristic of instructional conversations, which might take place utilizing more than one language, is their didactic purpose. In guiding learners to achieve the lesson goals within a specified time frame, however, our mindset/feeling can easily reflect the notion that there are not enough hours in the day to release learners to hold ongoing conversations. This fear of falling behind often puts us on the road to a more traditional way of questioning and holding instructional conversations that sometimes feels like a one-way street. We attempt a quick check for understanding by

posing a question and hands go up. The answer is confirmed or disconfirmed and the lesson continues. This limited initiation-response-evaluation pattern of interaction does little to respond to the individual needs of exceptional CLD learners and fails to engage students as active, critically thinking participants in the knowledge construction process. Even when we incorporate a quick think-pair-share, our overriding focus is often about getting back to the lesson.

Creating the dialogic type of communicative exchanges that we seek takes reconceptualizing teacher–student interactions. We teachers bring many assets to the teaching and learning process, including knowledge of the content, an understanding of the curriculum and larger educational system, methods and strategies for teaching, and our own lived experiences. Together, these represent the "official space" of the classroom (Gutiérrez et al., 2003). Students also bring ideas about the curriculum, schooling, and their own background knowledge and experiences. Yet their thoughts and experiences, described as the "unofficial space" (Gutiérrez et al., 2003), frequently remain merely an undercurrent in the classroom, bubbling beneath the surface, an unrecognized source of ideas and energy. What results situationally as the lesson unfolds during work time is a disconnect between learners and instruction.

For the learner in RTI tiers and/or prereferral/referral or receiving services, those situational moments that foster connections between the known and the unknown are critical to core instruction. It is in these moments that we want the learner's brain to fire up and engage in the learning. However, unless we "tune in" to and use what is being produced and made public, the learner is likely to remain disconnected or exhibit challenges with behavior, as students perceive their knowledge and ideas to have no real value or bearing on the lesson, and they see few (if any) opportunities to play an agentic role in their own learning. Yet students' expertise and thinking can be maximized *toward* learning if they are brought into play. When we draw upon the assets of both teachers and learners, we create new possibilities for learning in what has been termed the "third space" (e.g., Bhabha, 1994; Gutiérrez, 2008; Gutierrez et al., 1995).

In the third space, teaching and learning become a reciprocal exchange. The teacher(s) and learners all contribute toward the collective learning processes of the classroom community. This type of interaction requires give and take on the part of all involved. In the third space, the teacher and students work together to engage with the content, contributing ideas, asking questions, sharing perspectives, and exploring how the curriculum aligns (or fails to align) with their knowledge, language, and lived experiences. Revoicing what learners produce and explicitly making connections to home, community, and individual experiences become a standard part of learning in classrooms that foster JPA in the third space (Herrera, 2022). Creating that third space where the native language and culturally bound knowledge and life experiences are recognized and utilized to build toward the learning goal is critical during core instruction for both the CLD learner who is in the referral process and those receiving services. Content/conceptual knowledges lives in the words and experiences that CLD learners bring from home and community. Through instructional conversations, we as educators artfully foster the third space and attend to what students produce in order to weave their ideas into an interactive, collaborative telling of the lesson's story.

The following excerpt of instructional conversation illustrates the ebb and flow of student and teacher talk that is typical of the third space (Holmes, 2022). The 4th-grade teacher is working with a small group of learners to read and make sense of a passage in the text about the Louisiana Territory. Earlier in the lesson, learners used individual Vocabulary Quilts (see overview in Appendix A) to document their initial connections to the vocabulary terms. Now, after encountering the word *territory* in the text, they are discussing what they recorded for the word on their quilts.

> *Marcos:* I just draw . . . a little hut, and then I draw, I tried to draw, um. (teacher leans in to focus on Marcos)
>
> *Teacher:* And why did you draw that? What were you (makes a circular motion with her hand near her head) thinking?

> *Marcos:* What I was thinking, of, like . . . guarding a territory so. . . .
>
> *Teacher:* So, like they were guarding their . . . (pauses for students to join in).
>
> *Jasmine:* Land.
>
> *Teacher:* Land, right? So that word "land" (points to Hector's paper) is really what that territory or territories. . . .
>
> *Victor:* Land is territories.
>
> *Teacher:* But what does, is it just any land? (directs question to Victor)
>
> *Hector:* (shakes his head)
>
> *Patricia:* No. (shakes her head)
>
> *Victor:* It's your land.
>
> *Teacher:* The land that you (pauses for students to join in)
>
> *Students:* Own.
>
> *Teacher:* Okay, maybe you need to add that then to that box there, right? (addressed to all students, indicating the relevant box on the Vocabulary Quilt) It's not just any land, but it's going to be the land that you (pauses for students to join in)
>
> *Students:* Own.
>
> *Jasmine:* Land that you own. (moves to write on her tool)
>
> *Teacher:* Or land that you own. Or certain land. (students all write on their tools)

In this excerpt, we see the teacher respond to Marcos's illustration of a hut by eliciting his rationale for the connection. She then revoices his word *guarding* and uses it to prompt the group to consider what a person might guard. Jasmine offers the word *land*. The teacher immediately uses her word to prompt deeper thought about what characterizes such land. When Victor moves the conversation toward the idea of possession ("It's *your* land."), the teacher builds on that idea to lead learners to the word *own*. She then supports learners in using their tool in the hand to capture their evolving thought about the concept of territory, reminding them to add the word *own* to their Vocabulary Quilts.

In this exchange, the teacher does not, strictly speaking, provide the learners with the definition of territory. Rather, they construct their definition of the word together. The background knowledge connections that all students recorded on their tool in the hand served as catalysts for what they shared in this conversation. All learners participated in the dialogue. Most used spoken words; however, non-verbal responses were also part of the conversation. As the dialogue continued, the Vocabulary Quilt allowed all students to document their new understandings about the vocabulary word. Although this excerpt is just a sliver of the conversation that took place, we can see how the teacher allowed learning to unfold naturally. She used what students produced to gradually build toward the desired level of understanding.

When asked about this particular episode of instructional conversation, the teacher shared the following:

> [Y]ou can probably hear and tell, but I drive the conversation from their ideas. Everything is driven from what they say. And then I kind of add to it, and then another kid pops in. . . . And then I give them something else to ponder and think about. . . . They truly feel like they're a part of the learning and *they are the learning*. . . . I just basically started the conversation with, "What did you draw for territory?" you know, and then let you [students] lead from that. (Holmes, 2022, pp. 153–154)

The teacher highlighted how she uses what students say to drive the conversation. For this to happen, teachers have to give students opportunities to document their ideas; share their ideas; and engage in a natural, collaborative exchange of ideas about the content. Instructional conversations of this kind are not scripted. Although we often include opportunities for small-group conversations in our lesson plans, we cannot know in advance how they will unfold. Instead, we as teachers must be ready to attend situationally to what learners do and say in order to creatively use their words and ideas to stretch their thinking, advance their conceptual understanding, and support their ongoing language and literacy development. For the CLD learner whose culture and language is not the dominant culture and language of the classroom, it is especially imperative that core instruction and services be grounded in and guided by what is produced (assets bound) as the lesson unfolds.

Learning in Action Feature 5.2

This learner uses the Vocabulary Quilt to record her connections to the lesson's vocabulary words.

Students use their quilts as scaffolds to support their learning and engagement in the small-group instructional conversation.

Questions to Consider

Why is "tuning in" situationally, during core instruction, critical to the CLD learner who has been referred for evaluation and to those receiving services in your classroom? What role do instructional conversations have in creating a third space?

COLLABORATION: AFFIRMATION AS EQUITY

Each learner brings words, ideas, and experiences to the classroom that can be leveraged to support their own learning and that of their peers. Yet CLD learners, especially those who have been referred and those receiving services, may struggle to engage in the unscaffolded oral language of the typical classroom. As a result, their voices are rarely heard and they easily become part of the backdrop to conversations rather than active participants in exchanges. In such scenarios, opportunities for affirmation of strengths often go unnoticed. When the assets and ideas of CLD learners are unnoticed by their peers, this contributes to students' feelings of insignificance and their relative invisibility in the classroom. By contrast, conversations that are grounded in and guided by the learner's biography (Herrera, 2022) provide the teacher with concrete evidence of what has been produced throughout the lesson. This serves as the source of affirmation for the learner and information for the teacher to advance the lesson.

Equity is found in instruction and evaluation when the teacher can provide the assessment team with the challenges, but also evidence of the strengths drawn from the CLD learner's native language, knowledge, experiences, and gains witnessed during instructional conversations or from what has been documented on a tool in the hand. Using hands-on tools, such as those included with BDI strategies, ensures that each learner can write or draw ideas that then become the catalyst for engaging both socially and academically in talk. This scaffolding is pivotal for CLD learners in the referral process and those receiving services.

Teachers set the stage for equity in the classroom by affirming and modeling what it means to collectively create a space where all students have the opportunity to articulate their views. Those views are revoiced, documented, and utilized throughout the lesson and ultimately become the source of affirmation at the end of the lesson. Such actions demonstrate in practice what it looks like to listen *with the intent to understand* and to celebrate *all production* by *every learner* in the classroom. Teachers model for students by valuing and incorporating others' perspectives and celebrating with the community the power of both the individual and the collective. They thereby ensure that the ecology of the classroom is one of acceptance, respect, and trust for all.

Consider how the 1st-grade teacher in this excerpt interceded to ensure that Mia, one of the small-group members, was able to engage as an equal member of the team. In this exchange, each learner was selecting a commonality among ideas on a Linking Language poster and gaining the teacher's approval to physically link the ideas by drawing lines to connect same/similar words and pictures. When finished with linking, the learners were then supposed to record their idea on a sticky note and attach it to the poster.

> *Teacher:* All right, this poster. What did you see that you want to link? (stoops down toward Mia)
>
> *Mia:* I want to link. . . .
>
> *Michael:* (interrupting) I want. . . .
>
> *Teacher:* Oh, it's Mia's turn. (speaks to Mia) What did you see that is similar? What is the same?
>
> *Mia:* Um, the girls and boys.
>
> *Teacher:* The girls and boys (points to the poster) that are on there? (gives Mia a sticky note)
>
> *Kevin:* Wait! I was gonna link the girls.
>
> *Teacher:* Well, she's got the girls and the boys. (indicates Mia) What would you (indicates Kevin) like to link?
>
> *Mia:* (looks up questioningly at the teacher) And I'm going to link (indicates poster) all the girls and the boys?
>
> *Teacher:* Mm-hm. And then label your sticky note.
>
> *Kevin:* The unicycles.
>
> *Teacher:* The unicycle (indicates poster), the guy on the unicycle. (hands sticky note to Kevin) Okay, can you circle all of those and link them for me? And then label your sticky note.

In this excerpt, we see how the teacher reinstated Mia as the speaker after Michael interrupted her. The teacher also settled the disagreement about who got to link the concept of girls, stating that Mia was going to link both the girls and the boys. These teacher actions reaffirmed the status of Mia as an equal contributor in the conversation and in the overall learning processes of the group (Holmes, 2022). It is through teachers' attentiveness and responsiveness that collaboration and talk during core instruction elevate the most vulnerable learner to the space where their voice is equal to that of everyone else's in the classroom.

Questions to Consider

How do you ensure that all learners have equitable opportunities to participate in classroom conversations and activities? What threats to such equity currently exist? How does the closing of the lesson bring all the stories together to affirm the voices of the community?

One of the most important ways that we as teachers bring exceptional learners into the life of the classroom is by highlighting their assets and contributions for the classroom community. Using their words and ideas to support the learning of the rest of the class demonstrates to their peers that they are equally valued members. As one teacher reflected on her classroom practices, she discussed how socioemotional factors influence her decisions about which words from students to revoice and highlight in her instructional conversations with the whole group. In this case, learners had used DOTS charts to make connections to their background knowledge. They then had discussed their connections with their teammates before the teacher brought the class together for a whole-group discussion.

One of my most favorite things to do was to walk around and gather the students' ideas so that the words that . . . I was using, that the class was using [in the instructional conversation], were, they were knowing they were coming from their peers versus me. And I also really enjoy like *saying* the person's name that it came from. . . . A lot of the kids' names I purposefully said [during the conversation] are more of the kids that maybe *don't* have a lot of things to share often, or are a little bit *lacking* in the academic spectrum, or, you know, just have maybe not a great attitude about learning or not as, you know, like gungho about doing all these fun activities. . . . When kids don't feel like they belong, they shut out, they shut down. . . . [I]f you walk around and you gather each

kid's ideas . . . and then you say like, "Oh, [student name] shared this word. I thought that was great," and I mean like, you're bringing them *in* to the classroom and you're making them feel like, "Oh, wow! I contributed something," like "*I* contributed that to my class. *I'm* doing that." So, you're really giving them the sense of *belonging* and like . . . "*I'm* important. My class *needs* me." (Holmes, 2022, pp. 145–146)

Within the classroom community all actors must be positioned to be affirmed throughout the lesson. Conversations that spring from the community have the potential to support learners in making public knowledge, skills, and experiences that otherwise will be left untapped. Student agency is fueled by the teacher's affirmation of products that exemplify a learner's contributions (Wormeli, n.d.). CLD learners who have been referred for evaluation or are receiving services often are not provided the opportunity to become engaged participants in learning on their own terms. We as teachers have the power to position all learners as knowledgeable, capable, and valued members of the classroom community.

AGENCY "I": CONTEXT, CONDITIONS, AND SITUATIONS

Part of what it means to be in community with others is to care about their success and well-being. In culturally responsive classrooms, teachers work to build a shared culture of caring, sharing, collaboration, and respect. We accomplish more by working together than any one of us can do alone. This means that we need to find ways to maximize the expertise, cognition, and synergy within the classroom. We need to make the words and ideas of each learner available to the larger community (Pontier & Gort, 2016). This way, all students are able to benefit from the wealth of assets collectively possessed by the group of learners.

One of the most common ways that teachers do this is by displaying a class version of the BDI tool in the hand. As students share ideas, and as key concepts are encountered in the lesson, the teacher models how to add words/images and link ideas. This modeling provides additional opportunities to demonstrate how language is used and to engage learners in conversation. Teachers can ask students to re-explain the rationale for their connections, or they might encourage learners to find links between the ideas contributed by their peers. When teachers question to probe for understanding, learners then have their individual tools in the hand as well as the class version to use as resources.

All these layers of scaffolding and support work together to ensure that every CLD leaner, including those who are receiving RTI, have been referred, or are receiving services, are able to reach their full potential. As their words and ideas become part of the fabric of the classroom, they gain an increased sense of belonging and competence. Each success, no matter how large or small, builds their confidence that they *can* achieve the learning goals and that they, too, have something valuable to contribute. By utilizing instructional conversations to bring *all* learners into the third space, teachers create classroom conditions that honor and maximize the unique human potential of each learner and support all to contribute as equal, valued members in the learning community.

CONCLUSION

Students take their cue from us. They observe our words and actions to determine what weight we place on the contributions of each learner, and what expectations we have for each learner's success. Our diligent observations and purposeful decisions about how to involve learners in the JPA of the classroom are pivotal to creating an inclusive classroom community. In this chapter, we explored what culturally and linguistically responsive instructional conversations sound like in classroom practice. The examples provided illustrated multiple factors that teachers consider as they engage with learners as the lesson unfolds. Teachers provided multiple entry points to the lesson's content, as well as multiple ways for learners to demonstrate and document their knowledge, skills, and ideas. They also responded situationally to what learners were producing in the moment, so they could use students' words and illustrations as a springboard for academic conversations. They fostered equitable turn-taking and used their instructional conversations to affirm the contributions of all learners, especially those who might benefit most from having their ideas highlighted for the rest of the classroom community. Ultimately, this chapter demonstrated that by engaging with students in the third space, we can create classroom contexts where all CLD learners feel empowered and supported to make the learning process their own.

CHAPTER 5 QUESTIONS FOR REFLECTION AND DISCUSSION

As educators, the first step toward undoing, rethinking, and reimagining is to reflect upon the three C's—challenges, caveats, and considerations—that impact our practices. As professionals in a field that has so many competing agendas, it is critical to reflect upon about our views and perspectives and the role we play in making a difference in the lives of students and families. Reflect on this chapter and independently or collectively with a team, take a position on how you would respond to the following questions.

Challenges

1. How can grouping configurations be used to provide accommodated instruction and foster student talk in diverse classrooms?
2. How does the biography of the learner become core to ensuring equity in educational contexts?

Caveats

1. How do educators accommodate and let go of deeply embedded assumptions of learners' ability to participate given language proficiency?
2. How will situational formative assessments and post-instructional assessments reflect conditions present during instruction?

Considerations

1. In what ways does social-emotional learning intersect with biography-driven instruction?
2. How will instructional conversations using the learner's full linguistic repertoire be used to ensure equity and access during instruction?

Part III

REIMAGINING EQUITY FOR ALL LEARNERS

CHAPTER 6

Real-Life Language Development
A Bridge for Inclusive Classrooms

All year he's been struggling with reading and even opening up in class and sharing. I think it's been amazing watching him grow. And looking at him, and actually him turning and discussing. . . . Like we were talking about career choices and I think, again, we were using Vocabulary Quilts and some of that, and him then sharing what he wants to be. And then not only that, but him being able to generate—because he had that tool in his hand—him being able to generate a whole sentence about that, without using a sentence starter or anything, but just on his own, just because he has those tools, was just like amazing!

—Natalie Armijo, 3rd-Grade Teacher

Note the unfolding of content- and socially driven language observed by the classroom teacher in the opening excerpt. Now consider the contrast between that perspective and the view of the following special education teacher regarding her role to support *access* to the curriculum.

All I do is phonics all day long. I don't do comprehension. Then I have my math group. It's hard for me to use BDI, because a lot of it [BDI] seems like it's for comprehension.

What do we mean by curriculum? Is it just decoding of calculations or the printed word? Is that enough to ensure equitable access in education? What happens when "specialized supports" equate only with remediation of *deficits*, holes that can be filled in isolation via scripted curricula? What more could be gained by supporting students' engagement in, or development of, their own community of learners? How do we set those conditions?

In recognition of this potential, much of this chapter will be devoted to practical ways that common IEP goals for oral language can be powerfully addressed via BDI (Herrera, 2022). As throughout this text, the premise of BDI draws attention to the student's biography or personalized experiences and education. Culturally and linguistically diverse students do not become any less unique or diverse upon placement in special education. The very

presence of IEP goals related to speech and language indicate that, per law (IDEA, 2004), both *eligibility* and *need* for specialized instruction have been determined through culturally and linguistically appropriate processes. To be valid, these processes must be informed by the biography of the *individual* learner. Such evaluations may or may not include performance on static assessments, but statements of communicative ability should never be based on point-in-time snapshots of this dynamic human domain.

Ideally, our focus on language goals could presume consideration of the factors necessary to differentiate between

1. communication difficulties that can result from situational, experience, or measurement mismatch and
2. communication difficulties that persist across developmental timelines, contexts, and languages.

In other words, only those students with true communication disabilities should be placed in services for the "speech–language impaired" or labeled as having a "language-related disability."

Although this chapter is framed in terms of *oral language*, expressive language is not always oral. Many individuals and communities use manual or

71

sign language rather than, or in addition to, verbal language. Other forms of expression may involve picture/symbol selection or complex technologies to facilitate human-to-human sharing of information and ideas. Although detailed applications are beyond the scope of this text, readers are encouraged to consider the alignment of examples provided to the *communicative purpose* desired. In this manner, and with the input of related specialists (e.g., speech, occupational therapy, physical therapy, assistive technology, deaf education), minor adaptions can ensure the equitable engagement of every child's mind, heart, and "voice" (see Chapter 7 for discussion of accommodations for students with low-incidence disabilities).

Voices From the Field

When CLD learners qualify for special education services, I think it is important for special education and ESOL [English for speakers of other languages] staff to remember the importance of continuing to provide explicit and intentional language instruction. Language acquisition needs do not go away with the provision of special education services; these two areas should be overlapping and comprehensive in order to provide the most benefit to CLD learners.

—Meagan Montes-Murphy, Ed.S., School Psychologist

BDI AS TREATMENT CONTEXT

Significant research exists to support the benefits of home language maintenance and second language acquisition for emergent bilingual students in general and, more specifically, those with special education needs (Cleave et al., 2014; Gonzalez-Barrero & Nadig, 2017; Rodríguez & Rodríguez, 2017; Thordardottir, 2010). BDI implementers also recognize that the opportunities inherent in *activation*, *connection*, and *affirmation* inspire content and language growth among all CLD students, including those with disabilities. Indeed, BDI affords the combination of individualization, reach, rigor, and relevance required to lessen the cultural/linguistic restrictiveness of any educational setting.

For practical usage, the remainder of this chapter is organized by common IEP goals in areas of

oral language. Each will be followed by a brief description, pertinent considerations, and examples of how teachers or specialists may address that area during implementation of a BDI strategy. We encourage teachers of students with specified goals, as well as those suspecting *need*, to note the natural interface between BDI and best practices for targeting language. Because CLD students with disabilities do not cease to also be impacted by instructional, linguistic, and experiential differences, BDI-guided practices also reduce the harm caused by either/or thinking ("Is it learning or language?") that can arise during referral. (*Pro Tip:* The answer to that question is always "Yes.")

Students who have speech or language disabilities will often have an IEP goal to:

- Increase intelligibility or improve production of speech sounds
- Increase expressive language (quantity, use, structure)
- Expand content understandings/use (vocabulary, semantics)
- Demonstrate comprehension (content, directions)
- Ask questions for a purpose (seek clarification, obtain information)
- Answer questions to affirm or explain understandings
- Retell a story or personally experienced event
- Summarize a story or text
- Increase speech fluency (reduction of disfluent or "stuttered" speech)

Each of the areas listed above represents a broad continuum of skills. The starting point or baseline for each student is based on their present levels and strengths—what that student can or does do. The degree to which this is considered a "disability" must be heavily informed by the student's personal biography.

The target goal should indicate a point of progress or advancement along the continuum described, contextualized by the life of the student. The most successful and rewarding IEPs describe the whole student and envision skill development across multiple contexts. It is not enough to write a goal for how one might score on a point-in-time test. In the sections that follow, we offer a brief description of the language targeted by each type of goal, how it might be addressed through BDI, and ideas for measurement of success.

Goal: Increase Intelligibility or Improve Production of Speech Sounds

Students with an IEP goal for **articulation** (the production of sounds) or **phonology** (e.g., producing a sound located in different positions within words) have difficulties producing sounds in speech. Not all languages use the same sounds, but there is often correspondence in the types of errors noted across languages. For example, the student who substitutes /t/ for /k/ may say "tar" for car and "tee" for key in English. When asked for home examples, the parent may report pronunciations like "titab" for 'kitab' in Arabic or "tama" for 'cama' in Spanish. Figure 6.1 provides additional examples.

In these cases, remediation may be quicker when practice words and activities occur in both languages (Fabiano-Smith & Goldstein, 2010). We want the words to be relevant regardless of language. This can be accomplished by periodic parent consultation and harvesting examples of errored words from that setting. The speech-language pathologist (SLP) can then demonstrate how to practice the sound(s) or word(s) at home to ensure a *biography-centered* approach to remediation. Teachers can collaborate with the speech-language pathologist to share examples of successes and words to target that are heavily used in class. Names of friends and preferred activities are often among the most potent for increasing feelings of success with speech.

Figure 6.1. Examples of Difficulties With Articulation or Phonology

Parent	Student
• hakaka	• hatata
• niktib	• nitib
• cartable	• atable
• macarona	• carrona
• gom	• dom
• casscroutte	• tastroute
• taswira	• swira

Sometimes the sounds or sound patterns a student has trouble with do not exist or are not used in quite the same way in both languages. In either case, the school speech-language pathologist will develop a plan to remediate errors deemed "educationally significant." *Caution:* This may lead to inadvertent exclusion of the home language. Unfortunately, disregard for speech outside of school still has effects on in-school communication. Unaddressed difficulties in the L1 (first language) can increase self-consciousness about talking overall, self-esteem issues, reluctance to speak the home language, and reduced risk-taking in the L2 (second language). Failing to attend to L1 difficulties may also factor into language loss and diminished opportunities for the learner to maintain and grow socially and linguistically across all contexts. Although most teachers cannot directly impact home language growth, use of BDI with its validation of home language words, experiences, and conversations has the capacity to inform and enrich every aspect of communication at school.

Goal: Increase Expressive Language

This goal may be written in terms of the student's utterance length (i.e., number of words strung together) or an expansion of utterance type (i.e., words > phrases > sentences). Expressive goals may also be written to increase the student's use of specific elements (e.g., modifiers), structures (e.g., prepositional phrases), or basic functionality for expression of wants, needs, and joy. When expressive language is reduced, parents will report that their child speaks few words or has a limited utterance length at home, regardless of language(s). Sometimes this is referred to as "telegraphic" speech. Basically, the speech reflects only the bones of what the child wants to say. Reduced expression can be functional but impedes communication by requiring others to fill in or intuit messages based on context. For example, "Yadi ball hit" could mean that Yadi hit a ball, Yadi was hit by a ball, or Yadi hit someone with a ball. A child with truly affected language will have difficulty communicating effectively in *any language or setting*.

For older students, disabilities in expressive language may be less obvious, but they still will be characterized by insufficient detail to avoid misunderstanding or frequent need for listener clarification. The listener will have to work harder to get the message straight. Again, this challenge will be noted across settings, languages, and topics. If it is only noticeable in school, or when the student is constrained to one language, much more consideration should be given the variables summarized in Figure 6.2.

Speech-language pathologists who specialize in language frequently espouse modeling, revoicing, and clarification in natural contexts to expand student expression. Indeed, the challenge for SLPs in pull-out programs is how to create those natural contexts under the artificial conditions of that model. Increasing numbers of special education providers report that the opportunity to consult with classroom teachers using BDI is one of the most satisfying and effective ways to ensure targeted language growth among students with special needs.

Fundamental to every BDI-informed lesson is the activation and valuing of what individual students bring to the learning topic/experience. This becomes the Velcro onto which new learning and language are attached. Depending on the student, the expressive language brought forth may range from pictures (representational language) to spoken words, to elaborate ideas in the home language that cannot (yet) be expressed in the L2. These are the active ingredients, or "starter dough," that language teachers leaven through modeling, revoicing, and clarification of student-generated ideas.

Modeling occurs whenever there is genuine interaction. How can we ensure those opportunities exist within our classrooms and lessons? Many scripted programs or routines require students to recite or repeat words out of context. This may invoke mimicry, but that differs from modeling. Effective modeling involves frequent use of a word or sentence pattern while conversing about or explaining something of interest to the listener. Consider the following example.

> *Student:* Bingo!
> *Teacher:* Yay! What kind of row is it? *Vertical* (holds arm straight up), *horizontal* (positions arm across chest), or *diagonal* (tilts arm accordingly)?

Figure 6.2. Factors for Consideration With CLD Learners

Factors that may impact language development to a degree that a student requires specialized supports or modifications for educational access:

- Physiological phenomena that affect speech mechanisms, hearing, cognition, orientation to language as a social tool (e.g., autism spectrum disorder), auditory processing, etc.
- Psychological trauma or responses that interfere with interactive language development or use (e.g., selective mutism, isolation from human contact)

Factors that may impact home language maintenance:

- Positive parental and community support for home language maintenance
- Ongoing opportunities to hear and speak the home language in relevant contexts
- Ongoing opportunities to connect new learning with information, words, or language used outside of school contexts

Factors that may impact second language acquisition:

- Home language attrition while learning, and/or learning in, the L2
- Insufficient opportunities to interact with peers who are native speakers of the L2
- Segregated learning environments (e.g., English as a second language, special education) that reduce access to nondisabled and/or native English-speaking peers
- Instructional settings and approaches in which students are largely passive recipients of information

Factors that can impact performance on formal or informal assessment of language:

- Comparison of student language performance with dissimilar peers (e.g., assessments normed on monolinguals of any language)
- Probes of student's L1 and/or L2 under conditions that do not reflect the student's typical use of that language (e.g., unfamiliar people, settings, or purpose of task)
- Restriction to one language, and comparison of student performance in that language to that of monolingual speakers of either language, *regardless of language dominance*
- Reliance on oral or written responses to assess learning or knowledge

Student: Like this . . . berticle.

Teacher: Yuan got a vertical (gesture) bingo. Let's keep playing until someone gets a horizontal (gesture) and diagonal (gesture) bingo, too!

Revoicing is a way of restating, while validating or expanding upon, the message shared by a speaker. Revoicing can be used to clarify ideas or extend the thinking, syntax, or vocabulary used in the student's initial response. Revoicing depends on students having opportunities to talk and be heard. Consider how the teacher revoices in the following examples.

Example 1:

Student: My cry sad.

Teacher: I cry when I'm sad too. What makes you feel sad?

Example 2:

Student: (commenting on text picture of a lion) I have a cat, Dojo. He killed a bird.

Teacher: Did he hunt the bird like a *predator*?

Student: Yeah. He sneaked up on it, then . . . (jumps).

Teacher: So, first Dojo snuck up on his *prey,* the bird, then he pounced?

Student: Then he killed it, his prey, the bird was his prey.

Clarification occurs naturally when communicative partners sense a potential breakdown or misunderstanding of the message. The need to clarify increases as contextual clues and shared understandings decrease. This is why we use more detailed language in writing, or in situations where we cannot easily show or pick up on nonverbal cues that tell us we are on the same page when talking. Competent communicators use clarification strategies all the time. The following scenario illustrates clarification moves utilized by two students.

Student 1: He didn't want it so it didn't.

Partner: Who?

Student 1: The boy.

Partner: Oh yeah, Jack.

Student 1: Jack didn't want it.

Partner: What?

Student 1: The bike. Jack didn't want the bike. He wanted a scooter instead.

Partner: I'd rather have a bike.

Student 1: Me too.

There are numerous ways to engineer opportunities to build clarification. Among these are **information gap activities** that allow for clear and sometimes comical outcomes when critical information is omitted from a direction or message. For example, a student giving directions on how to make a peanut butter sandwich may tell the teacher, "Put peanut butter on the bread," to which the teacher responds by placing the jar of peanut butter on top of the loaf of bread. Visceral reactions to unintended outcomes (e.g., squashing the bread) lend immediate credence to the importance of seeking clarification. The most potent opportunities to model clarification, however, will occur when students have information of true personal value to share with teachers or peers. How often do we shut down comments we perceive as off-topic instead of eliciting clarification of how they may be connected in the child's mind? Knowing when, how, and with whom these techniques have special value requires us to know our students beyond the acronyms associated with special services.

Goal: Expand Vocabulary

This goal may be written in terms of a student's ability to demonstrate *understanding* of new vocabulary and/or *use* of more varied types of words. In all instances, words are best learned for their personal value. Words are tools. We choose the one best suited to get our ideas, wishes, or needs across in the most efficient manner. Words that make it easier to communicate about something that matters are more likely to become part of a person's personal dictionary or **lexicon**. The natural order of word learning is dictated by cultural and situational relevance (Hoff, 2006). This means that words learned first in one family frequently differ from "common" words in another. How might this impact our use of screeners or tests based on "words every child should know by the age of . . ."? When words selected for assessments do not reflect words commonly used in the student's community, those measures can lead to invalid perceptions of a student's ability to acquire vocabulary for school. Such tests reveal nothing about a student's lexical capacities or word learning skills (Peña et al., 2001).

Regardless of background, vocabulary is an area in which language grows continually throughout life. Sometimes the words are wholly new, such as those learned in specialized study (n: symbiosis; adj: phonemic) or those that are newly coined (v: MacGyver; n: GIF; adj: hangry, bingeable; n: mocktail). New words also include additional ways to use and interpret existing words given ever-evolving social forms (adj: *green* technology, "those kicks are *fire*," "nice *drip*").

Numerous BDI strategies specifically target vocabulary. Popular among these are Linking Language, Vocabulary Quilt, DOTS Chart, IDEA, and Word Drop (Herrera et al., 2011; Herrera et al., 2017). While these afford specific ways to build vocabulary, the Velcro hooks of any word become denser through exposure and use under any meaningful exchange. The beauty of BDI is that the starting point of instruction is always activation of what an individual brings to that lesson. We are inherently learning creatures, so readiness states and assets change daily. Knowledge not demonstrated on a preassessment is simply not yet learned or not yet ready to be demonstrated in the way it was measured.

Learning in Action Feature 6.1

Learners work collaboratively to discuss and document ideas on Vocabulary Quilt "blocks" related to the key vocabulary words of the lesson.

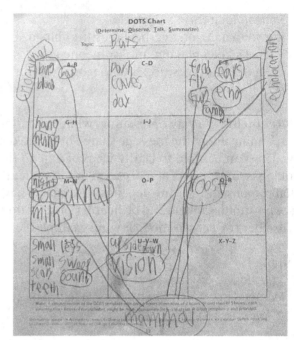

Note how many of the student's own words on this DOTS Chart became validated and consolidated into deepened grade-level vocabulary (e.g., echolocation, mammals, nocturnal).

Although adding content forms is crucial, some of the most important words in the English language are never found on traditional vocabulary lists. According to Anderson and Roit (1996), typical instruction for language minority students emphasizes high-frequency nouns, verbs, and adjectives but ignores vocabulary that "carries much of the logic of the language, for example, negatives, conjunctions, prepositions, and other abstract words" (p. 298). This statement mirrors our contention that the use of language targeted by language goals never occurs in isolation. Working on sentence elaboration and increased expression, regardless of word complexity, also benefits mastery of the vocabulary bits or glue that hold ideas about content together.

Goal: Comprehension of Content or Language

Comprehension goals may be written in a variety of ways. In all cases, the manner of showing comprehension should involve a strength or skill the student has already mastered. For example, asking a child with expressive weaknesses to demonstrate story comprehension by retelling a story will not permit insight into what the student truly understood, only what she or he is able to retell. The same caveats apply to the use of oral questions. Imagine the late scientist Stephen Hawking. Would his ability to answer questions verbally (without accommodative device) have been a valid way to measure comprehension? Clearly not. If, however, the goal is targeted to understanding question *forms*, such can also be probed without the need for verbal response.

Most common question types can be answered while pointing to pictures or words on BDI artifacts. Figure 6.3 illustrates how the Story Bag strategy (Herrera et al., 2017; see also Appendix A) can be used to elicit responses to different question types. Probing questions might include these:

- *Who* is the story/text about?
- *What* did [character name] do, find, feel, etc.?
- *Where* . . . ?

Teachers and student partners can then revoice the indicated answer in spoken words while affirming or refining the intended response. Students without a suitable word or depiction will often begin to add more detail when targeted questions are routinely posed or anticipated.

Another great strategy to probe comprehension is Listen, Sketch, Label (Herrera et al., 2011; Herrera et al., 2017). Instruction begins by activating and connecting student knowledge/language to desired aspects of the lesson (e.g., vocabulary, essential question, story setting). Students then listen to an orally read or spoken passage related to content. There typically is an opportunity to hear the passage again and discuss with a partner before creating one's own drawing of a visualized understanding. This strategy can easily be adapted to a range of comprehension levels or targets. After reading the richest version of a passage, the teacher may wish to provide select students with a more truncated version containing the same key content or highlighted

Figure 6.3. Using Story Bag to Probe Understanding of Question Types

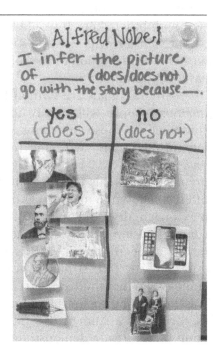

Students use the Story Bag strategy to make inferences about which people and objects will (or will not) appear in the story/text. Using visuals supports the teacher's ability to ask questions that range from identifying images that match the meaning of vocabulary words, to selecting the pictures that best match the topic of the text, to eliciting information about the text context. A larger version of the Story Bag chart supports class conversations about their predictions, which are revisited after the text is read to formatively assess comprehension.

aspect of language. For example, consider the following scenario:

> Marta has a goal to better understand or attend to describing words (adjectives). Although she hears the entire passage about Jaime missing the bus and finding a lost dog on his way to school, the teacher draws near to cue, "Jaime found a big, brown dog." Marta's picture will be as relevant to the story as others; however, comprehension will have been targeted toward, and then can be assessed relative to, her individualized need. Over time, Marta's teacher will add more detail to the rephrased version or build in opportunities to probe how she comprehends details after hearing only the original text.

BDI tools such as the Hearts template, Vocabulary Quilt, and Extension Wheel graphic organizer (Herrera et al., 2011; Herrera et al., 2017; see also Appendix A) also provide potent spaces for students to show comprehension of ideas, connections, and processes needed to develop academic schemas. The most important factor when probing comprehension is not to conflate comprehension with other skills. It would be invalid to assess comprehension with measures that require oral or written demonstration unless those are strength areas for the student.

Many IEP goals are written for "following directions." Some will specify the types of words contained in those directions. For instance, following directions "with the prepositions *in, on, under, behind*, etc." is really a goal to understand prepositions. Goals to follow multistep directions often boil down to memory. Our memory for complex or lengthy directions is only as good as our comprehension of the language plus memory for what has been spoken. This is not an easy task, especially for CLD students working in a second language. When multistep directions are targeted, it is imperative to first take an inventory of basic directions a student *does* follow. For example, Sonny has already demonstrated that he can follow numerous one-step directions, as indicated in Figure 6.4.

Using a short inventory of common classroom directions allows Sonny's teacher to more confidently probe his ability to follow multistep directions, such as these:

Figure 6.4. Documentation of Demonstrated Skills

Follow Oral Directions (circled observed):

Stand up Circle the ____ Turn off the lights

Find a toe partner Connect the ____ Close the door

High Five Color the ____ Fold your paper

Turn around Say your name Open the book

Draw a line Raise your hand Put your finger on ____

2 steps: Please <u>turn off the lights</u> and <u>close the door</u>. <u>Stand up</u> and <u>turn around</u>.
<u>Open the book</u> and <u>put your finger on a word</u>*.
3 steps: <u>Find a toe partner, high five,</u> and <u>say your name</u>.
<u>Turn your paper over, fold it hamburger style</u>* and <u>write your name on top</u>*
(*added concept complexity)

Although following multistep directions is a relatively common goal, we rarely are in situations where we need to follow more than three steps at a time. Comprehension complexity usually occurs at the level of challenging vocabulary and syntax. In the end, the value of any goal is the extent to which it improves one's function in school and life.

Thinking holistically, the ability to use contextual and social skills to enhance comprehension is the ideal. For that reason, probes and scaffolding opportunities in BDI lessons not only allow the teacher to maximize comprehension but also make every interaction within that setting simultaneously remediative and rich.

Goal: Ask Questions for a Purpose (e.g., Seek Clarification, Obtain Information)

Why is asking questions an important goal when what we really need is for students to "listen"? We're glad you asked! Sometimes questions are perceived, and responded to, as indicators that the student did not pay adequate attention "the first time." Conversely, questions by students in college are often perceived to signal engagement; such students may even be thought to have a stronger desire to deepen understanding than their quieter peers. As more and more students of all ages are being asked to consider essential questions, we must first acknowledge that questioning in general is essential. Questions are fundamental steps in the human communicative dance, regardless of setting. The next time you are on the phone with a close relative or friend, tally the number of times either of you advances the conversation with an interrogative (Huh? Who? When? You mean . . . ?). These forms are used to ask questions for information, seek affirmation of ideas, clarify understandings, or simply take a conversational turn. This is one of the reasons young children can drive adults a little crazy with the discovery that questions are, in fact, tools to keep others engaged.

Top educators value the ability of students to ask *good* questions while also affirming that "all questions are good questions." Bravo to whoever coined that phrase! In the hierarchy of question types, those that can be answered with "yes," "no," or facts at hand may be considered less demanding but are nevertheless potent ways to develop skills in the sociolinguistic space. Strategies to practice "right there" questions include any structure that enables students to pose and practice questions with varying partners. Thumb Challenge, Magic Books, and fact-filled Foldables (Herrera et al., 2011; Herrera et al., 2017) are among the tools that can be used to scaffold asking (and answering) lower-level questions to multiple peers. With each exchange, students become more adept at forming the question while also learning to adjust wording to the affective state and language proficiencies of the recipient.

Many BDI strategies, such as U-C-ME and Active Bookmarks (Herrera et al., 2011; Herrera et al., 2017), are also designed to help students formulate and document questions. These may arise during *activation*, including what a student would hope to learn more about, or as the *connections* are made to new content—prompting new associations, questions, or disconnects to resolve. Moving through the levels of TpsI, students gain more and more prowess in their abilities to interact with texts, topics, and people through their practice with formulating questions.

Goal: Answer Questions to Affirm or Explain Understandings

Readers will have already noted our cautions related to distinguishing verbal abilities from student demonstration of knowledge. Oral or written answers to oral or written questions are as much a probe of linguistic skills as they are of whatever content understandings and skills they are intended to assess. Teachers will therefore want to ask themselves, "What is the purpose of my question?" If the purpose is to *assess learning or knowledge*, how else might that be demonstrated? How else might the question be posed? If the purpose is to foster the ability to *recognize and respond to question forms*, we must ensure that the student is only being asked about information or experiences she or he already knows.

The order of difficulty varies, but goals for answering questions often include the following:

- Yes/no questions—In a nutshell, does the student reliably say "no" when they mean no, and "yes" when they mean yes? Such questions also can be effectively answered with gestures (e.g., thumbs up/down, head nods/shakes) or intonational responses (e.g., "um hmm," "uh uh").
- Basic 'Wh' questions—Does the student understand that *who* generally refers to a person, *what* a topic or item, what someone/something is *doing* an ongoing action, and *where* a place? Many times, *who*, *what*, and *where* questions can also be answered by indicating a corresponding picture, word, or action until students are comfortably ready to speak.
- *Why* (cause and effect) or *how* (procedural) questions—These questions seek insight into a process or connection. Answers to these types of questions require more verbal elaboration, but the ideas can also be conveyed through demonstration, drawings, arrangement of pictured events/steps, and/or connected elements on a tool in the hand.

Teachers need not worry that acceptance of modified responses will discourage language use or development. Indeed, gestures often facilitate language (LeBarton et al., 2015). Rather than lowering expectations, the use of accommodations improves teachers' insight into student learning while also engineering opportunities to strengthen language through *modeling* and *revoicing* these powerful interactive forms.

Figure 6.5. Question Prompts to Utilize with BDI Strategies

What do you think of when you hear the word ____?
What picture do you have in mind?
What makes you think that?
What words did you connect on your DOTS Chart?
    Why did you connect ____ and ____?
How did you use your (DOTS Chart, Extension Wheel, Vocabulary Quilt, etc.) to answer the essential question?
Where did you find that information?
How would you summarize . . . ?
What else do you want to know?
Why did you draw/write/include . . . ?

Students who can already answer a variety of question types will be unlikely to have a goal or concern in this area. However, asking and answering questions helps all students think deeply about their own learning processes while engaged in BDI lessons. Figure 6.5 lists a variety of questions that teachers can use to foster language skills as learners engage with BDI strategies.

Goal: Retell an Event (Narrative Language)

This skill area allows students to not only demonstrate school skills (e.g., story grammar) but more importantly share personally experienced events with other people. The ability to tell what happened or craft a narrative is critical for students regardless of language(s) used, mode, or quantity of output. We all have a story to tell. From this perspective, any avenue that facilitates a student sharing, drawing, or talking about an event in their own lives will help us meet this goal.

Scaffolding this skill may be as simple as a paper folded in two. "First, this happened. Then this happened." Students unable to draw or speak the details could select among pictures or symbols to convey an important occurrence in their day or lives. Trifolds, quadfolds, and sequence panels can also be used to structure narratives, but not everyone perceives stories as linear events. For some, it is more of an unfolding or blossoming, while others might perceive a recirculating spiral over time (Herrera, Cabral, & Murry, 2020). As

followers of daytime dramas know, there rarely is just one storyline in life. It would be nearly impossible to tell what is happening on a favorite serial without appearing unable to stay on topic or efficiently get to the point. Characteristics that make a narrative effective depend greatly on setting, audience, purpose, and expectations for what constitutes a "good" story. Some of the most detailed and evocative narratives might occur first as chaotically exploding Mind Maps or back-to-front Mini-Novelas (Herrera et al., 2011; Herrera et al., 2017). There is, however, value in strengthening students' abilities to recognize key features of stories and use organizational frameworks to assist in retelling not only fiction but also historic events of the world.

Teachers are encouraged to consider the power of stories to capture the attention of students in every grade. For example, the Story Bag strategy (Herrera et al., 2017) is a fantastic way to engage young learners in the anticipation of story elements, characters, settings, problems, and outcomes of a new book or text. Students predict which pictured features will be in the story, pausing to discuss reasons and rationales with peers along the way. Interest is piqued and comprehension bolstered during times when learners read or hear the anticipated story. This strategy provides opportunities to check, revise, and retell narratives to better fit what the actual text revealed. Story Bag approaches provide natural opportunities for learners to make inferences, predict outcomes, use targeted vocabulary, justify opinions, and check understandings. They are fun, purposeful, and need not be limited to younger students.

Questions to Consider

How might Story Bag be used to advance learning and narrative ability in a secondary class such as English Literature, U.S. History, or Science (Geology, Biology, etc.)? How many students might predict, for example, that dinosaurs appear in the text chapter on Early Man?

There is no limit to the ways in which BDI strategies can be adapted to emphasize narrative flow.

Narratives are the way we explain cause and effect as well as sequences of events. Narratives persuade and inform. Narratives explain and invite retelling from another perspective, becoming contexts for dialogue.

Many times, a retelling goal is posed as a precursor to developing original stories, but retelling can be a more difficult task. Story retelling is essentially event retelling *and* expressive language combined *with* comprehension *plus* verbal memory. Before assessing a learner's ability to retell, creatively probe comprehension of content. It may be that the student *does* comprehend but lacks the cohesiveness or expressive skills to restate in the desired manner. If comprehension is a factor, oral retelling may not be the appropriate goal.

Goal: Summarize a Story or Text

Summarization is the ability to provide an objective overview or restatement of a story, text, or presentation. In school contexts, summaries are typically oral or written products used to demonstrate student comprehension of the main ideas and concluding message. An effective summary stays true to the source material while narrowing detail to its most important elements.

Tasks that involve summarization can be a challenge because the outcome requires comprehension (oral, reading), as well as the ability to see how all the parts hang together in order to determine the main points—as they relate to context. Whew! That is a lot. On that note, the ability to summarize may be intrinsically well developed in an otherwise inexpressive student. Possible ways to assess and validate these skills include having the student do one or more of the following:

- Select which of four pictures best tells what the story (or text) is about.
- Select (if literate in the L1 or L2) which sentence best summarizes the targeted content.
- Assemble prewritten sentences to create a summary paragraph.
- Verbally summarize what has been understood or heard in the L1 to a bilingual teacher or peer. Clarify meanings via the L1. Listen to that person's restatement in the L2, and "check off" on the interpretation.

Involving other students in the facilitation or creation of modification materials (e.g., visuals) simultaneously advances those students' skills to new levels while strengthening the concept of *summarization* for all.

Curriculum guides frequently foster student identification of main ideas by highlighting text. This works especially well for those who already recognize key ideas. How many times, however, do some students end up still unable to ferret out the main idea from their highlighter-soaked page? Teachers noting this outcome will often scaffold students' identification of the text's main ideas by working through paragraphs and pages together as a class. While beneficial for many, even this level of support can result in a string of inauthentically copied sentences to summarize a text the student still does not understand. This is also a problem with online summarizers designed to help students produce the summaries required by school. If the value of a summarization is its correlation with comprehension, the product needs to reflect the process, not the product.

BDI strategies are ideally suited to scaffold summarization processes. In nearly all instances, students document key elements of the topic/text in words or pictures that make sense *to them*. Understandings are enriched through partner conversations, instructional conversations, and evolving networks of connection. BDI strategies afford specific opportunities for students to develop oral or written sentences from words or pictures they have noted as relevant to their understanding of the material. In this way, tools such as DOTS Charts and U-C-ME or Extension Wheel graphic organizers (Herrera et al., 2011; Herrera et al., 2017) provide a natural scaffold of the concepts and language needed to form an oral or written summary on any topic.

Summarization skills are often depicted on charts and hierarchies as precursors to higher order applications that require synthesis of information or ideas. A synthesis is considered more complex than a summary because a synthesis requires one to consider the main ideas from more than one source or perspective. Complex conceptual processes are needed to compare, contrast, interpret, evaluate, and so forth, but these processes are occurring within us all the time. It is the difference between summarizing a movie and developing an

Learning in Action Feature 6.2

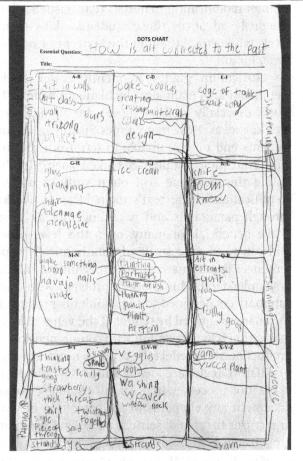

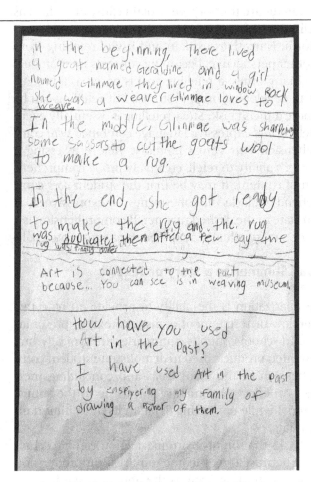

In these samples of 2nd-grade student work, the DOTS Chart served as a scaffold for the learner's individual summarization of the topic.

opinion about which character you liked best, or how the movie compared with the prequel. This is an easy line to blur during assessment but also a fantastic opportunity to see evidence of more advanced skills well before the curriculum asks students to synthesize findings, theories, or themes.

Goal: Increase Speech Fluency (i.e., Reduction of Disfluent or "Stuttered" Speech)

Students with a goal to increase "fluency" demonstrate disfluency or characteristics of stuttering. These speech qualities will be evident in each language, but not always in the same way. Fluency disorders affect oral speech but can also be factors in how students perform on tests of reading fluency, especially when timed or perceived as

high stakes. Students who stutter are often aware of words or sounds that will be harder to say. This may result in misread words or hesitations that make it appear the student does not decode with accuracy or at a rate associated with grade-level literacy.

When students have speech disfluency, it does not help to cut them off, fill in words, or advise them to "think first" or "slow down." Such attention to speech can actually increase tension. The student may feel there is more focus on *how* they talk than *what* they have to say. Positive ways to foster successful classroom climates for students who stutter include the following:

- Reduce verbal competition and interruptions. Partner and group sharing structures provide a natural environment to practice this important norm of communication.

- Model unhurried conversation. Be a patient listener. Show that you are focused on the content and message rather than the speech. Allow yourself wait time before answering students' questions. Include natural pauses in your own speech to recalibrate interactions that could otherwise feel rushed.

While recommended to enhance fluency, these are also the behaviors and social skills of effective communicators overall. The use of BDI strategies offers many benefits to teachers of students with a fluency goal. The opportunity to record ideas for reference during structured, positive interactions is among the most helpful to students in managing when and how they will respond to verbal prompts. Teachers are encouraged to learn more about their individual student's speech by consulting with the speech-language pathologist and parents. That said, the most salient aspect of BDI for students who stutter remains the consideration of each student's own biography and personal discovery of what works *for them*.

CONCLUSION

Students identified with "speech language impairment" demonstrate need(s) related to communication that are not attributable to cultural, linguistic, or experiential difference. The most common areas influencing school-aged children involve difficulties with articulation, speech fluency (e.g., stuttering), voice disorders, and language. Language is by far the broadest in scope. Language disorders or language/learning disabilities may include any combination of the receptive systems necessary for *comprehension* (e.g., vocabulary, memory, auditory processing, syntactic knowledge) and/or *expression* (words, sentence structure, message coherency). Such needs can also impact reading and writing. In these cases, the speech/language disability thought to impact literacy will be evident across languages and contexts. CLD students with speech/language impairments are at significant risk for misdiagnosis or oversimplification of needs. It is imperative to recognize these students' assets in order to appropriately identify needs and develop strengths-based plans for remediation of "weaknesses."

Language acquisition is always influenced, and therefore contextualized, by an individual's development, exposure, and experiences. All of the systems involved in this uniquely human skill require that innate ingredients be activated through social interaction. Language does not occur effectively outside of a communicative purpose. Because of this, use of instructional strategies such as BDI strategies enhances teachers' abilities to create opportunities in which cognitive linguistic "dough" is leavened and allowed to rise as a natural consequence of instructional opportunity.

CHAPTER 6 QUESTIONS FOR REFLECTION AND DISCUSSION

As educators, the first step toward undoing, rethinking, and reimagining is to reflect upon the three C's—challenges, caveats, and considerations—that impact our practices. As professionals in a field that has so many competing agendas, it is critical to reflect upon about our views and perspectives and the role we play in making a difference in the lives of students and families. Reflect on this chapter and independently or collectively with a team, take a position on how you would respond to the following questions.

Challenges

1. Why is it important to provide students non-verbal means to show learning and knowledge in general education and special education settings?
2. What questions and resources guide your school or district in determining the language(s) used during assessment of CLD students?

Caveats

1. Service intensity is often equated with group size. How might the larger numbers and fluid groupings available in inclusive settings be more beneficial to students with speech/language goals on their IEP?
2. How can you proactively address longstanding traditions of "pull-out" or "pull-to-the-back" services with general education and special education partners?

Considerations

1. In what ways can use of BDI strategies provide natural contexts for treatment of speech and language needs (IEP goals) within inclusive settings?
2. How will you use the information from this chapter to enhance students' language use throughout their engagement with the topics and activities of a typical school day?

CHAPTER 7

The Power of BDI for Students With Low-Incidence Disabilities

Even with my background, knowledge, and professional opinion I struggle to get through to some parents and teachers because this particular child isn't like "my friend's kid" or isn't like the student this teacher had last year with the same low-incidence disability which immediately leads to something being "wrong" with this child or a teacher putting this child to the side because "they can't do that anyways."

—Leslie D. Carreon, Speech-Language Pathologist

Families, teachers, and peers of students with less common disabilities can be particularly challenged by the needs of a child who appears so different from others encountered in school, in the community, or within the histories of cultural/familial knowledge. Why are some types of disabilities referred to as "categorical" or "low incidence"? How does this designation impact options and services for *CLD students* with a lower incidence disability? Does "lower incidence" presume higher needs? Does consideration of higher need in one area justify neglect of other aspects of a student's biography? In this chapter, we draw upon medical and social models of disability and then illuminate the promise of BDI practices to better meet the complex assets and needs of CLD students with disabilities who have traditionally been relegated to the most restrictive spaces in schools.

WHAT'S IN THE LABEL: CATEGORIZING THE CONTRADICTIONS

Disabilities are often categorized as high or low incidence, regardless of the linguistic or cultural backgrounds of students. For example, learning disabilities and speech–language impairments are considered higher incidence because they occur more often in school-age populations. Proportionally, more teachers will have had training and experience in methods to accommodate students with high-incidence needs. By contrast, IDEA Section 1462 (c) (3) describes "low incidence disability" in the following way:

(A) a visual or hearing impairment, or simultaneous visual and hearing impairments;
(B) a significant cognitive impairment; or
(C) any impairment for which a small number of personnel with highly specialized skills and knowledge are needed in order for children with that impairment to receive . . . a free appropriate public education.

All students must be recognized as uniquely faceted gems with their disabilities being a part of their biographical makeup. For those with labels (Figure 7.1 provides a quick reference for related acronyms and their meanings), this is but one aspect of who they are. Least restrictive environment (LRE) compels us to ensure inclusive spaces and instructional access for students with less common disabilities, such as those who are blind or vision impaired (BVI), are deaf or hard of hearing (DHH), have mobility issues, or are identified with multiple disabilities (MD).

Figure 7.1. Acronyms Commonly Used With Low-Incidence Disabilities

Key Terms and Acronyms
Assistive Technology—AT
Speech Language—SL
Blind or Visually Impaired—BVI
Deaf and Hard of Hearing—DHH
Orientation and Mobility—OM

Any discussion of accommodations for students with less common, or lower incidence, disabilities warrants consideration of the models that inform the interpretation of disability while focusing on the biopsychosocial histories of the learners. In the **medical model of disability**, profound sensory and mobility impairments are viewed as individually situated problems to be "fixed" or worked around for the affected person to participate in an "able-bodied" world. All related barriers, struggles, and conditions are therefore viewed as consequences of the disability.

In the **social model of disability**, it is not the person who is considered "broken" or fundamentally hindered by the disability. Barriers result instead from impediments to access created by **"ableist"** culture and design. For instance, an individual in a wheelchair encounters more barriers in a building with only stairs than in a building that also has ramps or elevators. The same person is therefore more "disabled" in negotiating and accessing resources in building A, and more "abled" in building B, despite no changes in their actual physical state. The social view of disability contends that a person with one condition or another is only disenfranchised from society to the extent that its systems and structures are based upon narrowed norms of ability. Hence, proponents of this model contend that disability is socially constructed.

Indeed, if every restaurant had Braille or voice-assisted menus, and every crosswalk beeped or vibrated when it was safe to cross, the differences labeled "disability" might cease to be quite so *disabling*. Those inclined to weigh accommodations with some metric of "cost" and "benefit" will be reassured by studies citing positive impacts to all when accessibility is increased for a few. For example, although closed captioning was designed to increase access for those with hearing impairments,

a recent study of university students found that 96.8% reported this accommodation as helpful to their own learning as well (Morris et al., 2016). Gernsbacher (2015) cites 100 empirical studies among varying groups indicating that video captions improve viewers' comprehension of, attention to, and memory of video content. Among the included studies were those measuring benefits for literacy development (Kothari & Takeda, 2000; Linebarger et al., 2010) and for learners of a new or subsequent language (Vanderplank, 2016). Closed captions help people who are deaf or hard of hearing but also those with auditory processing lags, age- or vocation-related hearing loss, and anyone hoping to enjoy content in a language they do not readily understand. Similarly, voice-activated features help the visually impaired, but also those with orthopedic impairments or arthritis, as well as the multitude of others who simply feel it is safer or more practical to use this feature while driving or managing another task.

An earlier study of pedestrian behavior at a shopping mall found that 9 out of 10 unencumbered pedestrians go out of their way to use a curb cut, the rounded or sloped sections of curbs designed to accommodate wheels (Greve, 2007). Curb cuts help people in wheelchairs, but also individuals using baby strollers, shopping carts, delivery trolleys, bicycles, and so forth. The potential for all to benefit from accommodations designed for a few is referred to as the **curb cut effect**. In short, everyone benefits when the world is more accessible. Yet, in the overall scheme of things, accessibility remains targeted toward the "disabled" and the resulting benefits that able-bodied individuals enjoy are essentially ignored. In much the same way, IDEA, along with Title VI, has provided certain safeguards for students with disabilities and for students who are learning a second language. Yet the accommodations needed for exceptional emergent bilingual students often go unrecognized in classrooms, even though everyone stands to benefit.

In response to these insights, educational approaches for students with disabilities have moved away from segregated places and "fixes" to improved access for all students across settings. Teachers and schools now are encouraged to accommodate students more proactively through **Universal Design for Learning (UDL)**. UDL is a concept advanced by the Center for Applied Special Technology (CAST). It is based on the principle that learning must be optimized through individuals' authentic access to the curriculum. The means by which UDL occurs are as individualized as the learners; however, proponents of UDL acknowledge three overarching modes of access. These include providing for

- **Multiple Means of Representation**— This entails thinking beyond the print or lecture format to consider other ways that information could be conveyed or experienced. How does the student take in information? This may require going beyond a surface-level translation, such as Braille or an audio reader. Could this student also receive inputs from realia or experience other representations of content (quantity/quality)? Might all students benefit from a sensory-rich experience related to descriptors, cause/effect, nature, physics, or art?
- **Multiple Means of Expression**—How do teachers create opportunities for and celebrate alternative ways students can demonstrate what they know and can do? There is really no end to the possibilities when teachers have a solid understanding of the content/skill learning objective. Complex knowledge can be just as powerfully demonstrated through advanced technological devices, simple arrangement of representative objects (e.g., base vs. alkaline, story components), or adapted performance of a procedure or script.
- **Multiple Means of Engagement**— How does the teacher account for the learner's experiences, strengths, attributes, and preferences to ensure interest and motivation? A well-written IEP will describe the student in enough individualized detail and contextualization to provide a great starting place for the development of a learning design *relevant to that student*.

Multiple means of representation, expression, and engagement are central tenets of Universal Design for Learning. Specialists in areas such as orientation and mobility (OM), deaf and hard of hearing (DHH), blind or visually impaired (BVI), and assistive technology (AT) will be valuable resources for planning universal access to the curriculum. According to UDL, the above layers of access exist at all four essential points of curricular accommodation: the instructional goals, use/choice of materials, implementation of methods, and planning for assessment. Effective application of UDL also compels recognition and affirmation of students' individual biographies (Fritzgerald, 2020; Torres & Rao, 2019).

Consider the impact of multiple means of representation, expression, and engagement for Rafi in the following vignette.

Rafi was in 1st grade at a dual language school in a Midwest town known for its teaching college and meat packing industry. To proactively address diversity, the school had implemented a 90/10 model whereby Spanish was the majority language and the language of literacy instruction in the early grades. Given the transparent or consistent nature of Spanish sound-to-symbol correspondence, most students found great success with learning to decode, regardless of home language.

Rafi, however, was different. He had trouble saying the sounds that the individual letters make, let alone understanding how they blended into syllables and words. These skills usually develop rapidly with mastery of even a few sounds in Spanish, so his bilingual teacher, Ms. Nova, was concerned. "No matter how much we practice and drill, Rafi either doesn't answer, says the wrong thing, or just repeats the last word someone else said. If I ask, 'What letter?', he'll say, 'What letter?' He's so low. All he ever wants to do is draw. Can we move him back to kindergarten? Or maybe he should spend the rest of this year in the ID (intellectual disability) room to see if he can learn there. Rafi is already in the lowest group but can't retain a thing." When asked about oral comprehension, Ms. Nova thought for a minute, "It's hard to tell because he doesn't answer questions."

As you reflect on the information provided about Rafi and his response to classroom instruction, what strikes you most about Rafi? What do you know? What do you not (yet) know?

Paying close attention to Ms. Nova's descriptions and responses, the teacher support team surmised that Rafi (circle all you agree with):

- Was not responding to the structured reading intervention (RTI)
- Did not accurately verbalize letter names, sounds, and printed words
- Could not decode or recognize 1st-grade words
- Did not reliably answer questions
- Would be more successful in a different type of class

Now, put an X over any circled items that are *inferred* from the observed behaviors, rather than descriptions of what Rafi *does*.

After a little discussion, the team realized that all they truly knew was that Rafi didn't use oral language in expected ways. Could it be that he knew more than he could show through verbal responses? How could they learn more about the reading skills he possessed?

Given Rafi's love of drawing, the speech-language pathologist suggested a way to probe reading through art. Ms. Nova would give Rafi a paper with the words *sol* (sun), *casa* (house), *mama*, and *gato* (cat) written in the four folded squares. Other students had different words. Students were asked to keep the words secret as they drew pictures in corresponding spaces of their page. These might become pictures for alphabet walls or sorting games, but her real agenda was to see if Rafi and one or two other learners could silently read any of the written words. Ms. Nova anticipated that Rafi would simply draw whatever he wanted but noticed that the first thing he drew in each quadrant represented the printed word. Then he added more and more details because, as previously mentioned, Rafi loved to draw.

Ms. Nova could not wait to find out what other words he might be able to read. That night, she created a sheet of 12 clipart pictures representing a variety of nouns, verbs, and adjectives. She made sure to include two words from the previous drawing page because he could read those, and she could use them to model the task. The next day Ms. Nova

showed Rafi the picture page. She wrote *sol* on a small sticky note and asked, "*¿Donde está el sol? Oh, aquí está* sol" (Where is the sun? Oh, here is the *sun*") putting the word "*sol*" on the small picture of a sun. She did this again with *gato*. Then she said, "*¿Donde está . . . ?*" to Rafi, handing him a sticky with the word *rojo* (red). He put it on the red circle. He did the same with *carro* (car), *ojo* (eye), *boca* (mouth), *comer* (to eat), *jugar* (to play), *verde* (green), *luna* (moon), *grande* (big), *fruta* (fruit), and *tres* (three). Ms. Nova was so excited! She snapped a photo of the page and shared it with the team.

Later that day during intervention, Rafi was asked to help with a special project. The reading teacher, Ms. Leo, told Rafi she was writing a children's story but needed an illustrator. Would Rafi mind helping with a book page while she worked with another group? Rafi was thrilled to get to draw "instead" of "do reading." Ms. Leo placed the paper in front of Rafi, "Draw something that goes along with the story here. Let me know if you have questions." At the top of the blank page the following lines were typed (excerpted from Casas & Portillo, 1992, p. 65):

> *Bernardo está en el zoológico. Los animales están en sus jaulas. Bernardo tiene una cámara para tomarle fotos a los animales. Bernardo ve a un tigre, un gorila, y un león. A Bernardo le gusta ir al zoológico.*

For readers unfamiliar with Spanish, are there any words you nevertheless recognize? How helpful is it to have literacy in your own language when trying to unpack words in another? Loosely translated, this passage reads:

> *Bernardo is at the zoo. The animals are in their cages.*
> *Bernardo has a camera to take pictures of the animals. Bernardo sees a tiger, a gorilla, and a lion. Bernardo likes to go to the zoo.*

Figure 7.2 provides the illustration that Rafi made. Now consider,

- What does Rafi's drawing say about his reading comprehension?

Figure 7.2. Rafi's Illustrated Response

Bernardo esta en el zoológico. Los animales están en sus jaulas. Bernardo tiene una cámara para tomarle fotos a los animales. Bernardo ve a un tigre, un gorila, y un león. A Bernardo le gusta ir al zoológico.

zoológico.

- How might this evidence inform decisions about the following?
  - » Return to kindergarten
  - » Placement in a classroom for intellectually disabled students
  - » Continued focus on phonics-based instruction
- Does Rafi appear to have an atypical disability in the area of expressive language?
- Does the team need to learn more to better understand Rafi's strengths and needs?

To the last question, we hope readers will respond with a resounding *Yes!* Rafi is learning . . . a lot. Let us not waste his time (or ours) training him to say what he knows in traditional ways. Yes, next-level phonics should probably be a component of his plan, but it need not be the primary focus. Continuing to follow a traditional approach to literacy instruction would serve only to limit his access.

Questions to Consider

The social model of disability compels us to address how social structures and perceptions shape the necessity for accommodations. A more contextualized view of disability requires us to be aware of and accountable for the mindsets behind deficit thinking

of any type. To this end: How does the district/ school educate stakeholders (e.g., administrators, teachers, support personnel, assistive technology/ speech language/deaf and hard of hearing/blind or visually impaired/orientation and mobility specialists, innovation partners) to address potential biases, misconceptions, and cultural blindness that foster barrier-thinking? How will the district/school empower parents and orient the work of stakeholders to identify and address situational, structural, or systemic barriers to inclusion at school as well as within the community?

SOCIAL MODEL OF DISABILITY, UDL, AND BDI

Readers likely will have already noticed similarities between the social model of disability, Universal Design for Learning (UDL), and biography-driven instruction (BDI). Each is based on the inherent premise that people, in this case students, have abilities we may never see or bring into learning unless the curriculum and structures are designed for all to participate and stakeholders reflect on the curriculum and instruction from a biopsychosocial lens. This is significant in that it calls out the inefficiency of retrofitting or tweaking "one size fits all" curricula to second guess *what* may work with *whom*. Instead, learning experiences are planned in ways that maximize access, interest, and inputs. As with UDL, BDI contends that the most powerful thing teachers can do instructionally is get to know their students. Implementers of BDI may refer to this as the biopsychosocial lens (see Chapter 3 for additional discussion of the biopsychosocial history of the learner).

Students with specific physical disabilities are just as diverse in terms of their (dis)ability histories as any other aspects of their individual biographies. All students with an identified disability, even within the same disability category, will not have had the same life experiences with that disability. For example, some BVI/DHH students will have been blind or deaf since birth. Others may have lost sight or hearing due to disease or accident, or they are experiencing progressive loss over time. Each will bring to the learning space their own assets and insights about how they learn best. It becomes our moral imperative to provide them with spaces in which these assets can bloom and take shape in such a way that their disability is not determined or increased as a byproduct of the environment we provide. It is then, and only within such spaces, that we can truly discover the best accommodations for each student. Given this understanding, accommodations to consider in BDI classrooms with students that have low-incidence disabilities include those listed in Figure 7.3.

Voices From the Field

As a special education teacher and a parent, I have found it easy to observe strengths and weaknesses in abilities. However, until recently I have not actively examined cultural differences, and honestly it [cultural diversity] is more prevalent than I had first thought, especially in rural Kansas. To put in perspective how I feel, it is like I have been walking down an alley and noticing the narrow path, but this whole time I have been missing out on the road and countryside right beside me. There are many ways I can support and talk with those around me if I embrace the differences rather than ignorantly ignore them. I continue to notice that the way we live, who we associate with, and how we show those around us they are important are based on our culture. . . . There have been situations I have reflected on with others, and I have noticed there may have been a better way, a stronger way to communicate if I had taken into consideration cultural differences. I am excited to continue learning and adapting my world view, my way of thinking, and how I teach and parent.

—High School Life Skills Teacher, Grades 9–12, Self-Contained Special Education

When it comes to accommodations, practicality matters as much as technology. Learning is not simply a byproduct of interactions that occur at school. Everyone benefits when students' biographical information obtained via families is maximized and, as a result, families end up becoming more aware and involved in the discovery and creation of effective accommodations. This provides them with additional ways to promote their child's access to learning. Their involvement also ensures that the selection and design of accommodations is informed by knowledge of the student's life, interests, and ecological adaptations developed over years of authentic interaction in the context of the home. Communication and accommodations for learning should be in a form or format that also can be utilized outside of school, or the student will be disenfranchised from learning within and from their own communities.

Key points to consider when engaging students with any kind of disability in classrooms where educators apply BDI principles include the following:

• Any time we create the conditions and situations that facilitate BDI, we are simultaneously incorporating the skills needed for *life*. All learners need opportunities to engage in conversations, draw upon their experiences, and meaningfully connect with content.
• Of the modifications described in this section, many can be readily adapted to, or facilitated by, the peer-to-peer interactions made possible through BDI.
• Flexible seating allows learners to benefit as much as possible from grouping configurations based on their biographies. Students can select the most advantageous position when working individually or within a pair, small team, or large group.

Planning for each student's participation and demonstration of learning will ensure that CLD learners with high- or low-incidence disability each have the same "ticket to ride" and available destinations as all other students. Figure 7.4 provides additional questions for educators to consider as they ensure the journey is a safe one for all.

CONCLUSION

Students with lower incidence disabilities are those who meet the IDEA criteria of having (1) a visual or hearing impairment, or simultaneous visual and hearing impairments; (2) a significant cognitive impairment; or (3) any impairment for which a small number of personnel with highly specialized skills and knowledge are needed for children with that impairment to receive a free and appropriate public education. Such factors do not define the student but are certainly components of an

Figure 7.3. Accommodations for Students With Low-Incidence Disabilities

Physical Disabilities

- Seating for groups and movement arrangements (e.g., virtual grouping, breakout rooms) that assure collaboration and/or sharing
- Alternative, augmented, or partner-facilitated scribing
- Alternative, augmented, or partner-facilitated drawing (pictures and/or connections)
- Opportunities for comment, question, and response selection (e.g., switches, buttons, technologies) for real-time engagement in discussion and when collaborating with peers
- Opportunities to visualize what is being shared around the classroom via projection methods, rolling easels, schema maps, etc.

Deaf and Hard of Hearing

- Attention to sound absorption materials on floors and walls (e.g., carpet, rugs, cork)
- Acoustic considerations for seating (e.g., vents, machine noise)
- Classroom sound distribution or "sound field" system
- Interpreter supports (e.g., American Sign Language, Signed Exact English, cued speech, oral language) that do not take the place of instruction but are used to *facilitate* student-to-student and teacher-to-student interactions
- Time for learners to process information
- Clear facial regard for speech reading
- Transparent face masks (when indicated)
- Comprehensible visuals (written or pictured)
- Use of digital devices (e.g., cameras) to transmit/collect concept and product ideas
- Frequent checks for understanding
- Alternate modes of assessment

Blind or Visually Impaired

- Orientation to room layout (and reorientation to changes)
- Large print
- Magnification devices (low and/or high tech) for viewing peer work
- Attention to color/contrast (e.g., may need to avoid orange, red, and yellow markers)
- Seating to maximize lighting (e.g., considerations for brightness and glare)
- Raised or perforated lines for mass-marketed images
- Media or materials to incorporate dimension and texture in art, images, or displays
- Real-time and/or technology-facilitated verbal description of visuals and visual aids
- Peers and teachers orally speak/read while writing on the board or adding to joint products
- Tactile representations (e.g., letters, objects, concepts)
- Realia or representative objects/forms to select, manipulate, arrange, and sort
- Voice-enabled timers, calculators, measuring tools, etc.
- Text-to-speech technologies (devices/apps), including those with optical character reader, voice output, Braille display, language translation, image description, and printer output

Multiple Disabilities

- Switches, buttons, and technologies to facilitate selection and expression
- Any of the above, as helpful for students who have concomitant disabilities such as deaf-blindness, physical and visual impairment, etc.
- Parent-informed accommodations that increase access to content and participation in the *most practical manner* available for the student

Figure 7.4. Questions for Promoting Safety in All Classrooms

Safety assurances for ALL:

- How will the student be made aware of critical alarms or alerts?
- Is the student able to distinguish the type of alarm and associate each with the recommended behavior or response (e.g., exit room, shelter in place)?
- Is each type of alarm or alert that occurs in the setting routinely included in all related practices and drills?

individual student's biography and biopsychosocial history. The lens of BDI allows teachers to see the disability as situated *within the life and experiences of the student*. The student is not the label. Students with the same label or disability can (and generally do) have vastly different experiences, both with the disability and with every other facet of life. CLD students with disabilities do not cease to be socially and linguistically rich upon categorization by need. Teachers who believe students' biographies can drive instruction will push against efforts to pick a single instructional lane (e.g., English for speakers of other languages, special education, "categorical") for CLD students with low-incidence disabilities, asking instead,

- How can we utilize student assets, paired with disability-related modifications, to create on-ramps to participation in the flow of engagement with others in the learning environment?

- How has our team considered the benefits of this student being able to access their primary language in each setting?
- How does denial of access to language supports in a special education context increase the *restrictiveness* of that setting?
- What might such considerations mean for this student's assurance of free and appropriate public education, as described in Chapter 2?

CHAPTER 7 QUESTIONS FOR REFLECTION AND DISCUSSION

As educators, the first step toward undoing, rethinking, and reimagining is to reflect upon the three C's—challenges, caveats, and considerations—that impact our practices. As professionals in a field that has so many competing agendas, it is critical to reflect upon about our views and perspectives and the role we play in making a difference in the lives of students and families. Reflect on this chapter and independently or collectively with a team, take a position on how you would respond to the following questions.

Challenges

1. How might the incidence (commonality) of a disability impact parents' and educators' expectations for students with exceptionalities?
2. What resources and expertise for supporting students with disabilities are present or needed in your setting?

Caveats

1. In what ways do the medical and/or social models of disability impact conversations around students?
2. Are there ways in which your life has been positively impacted by accommodations developed for persons with disabilities?

Considerations

1. What is the relationship between the curb cuts enabling equal access to physical planes (i.e., sidewalks) and use of BDI strategies to facilitate students' access to the heights of capability?
2. How will you use the information from this chapter to create spaces for new learning and practice with colleagues?

CHAPTER 8

Reframing Our Thoughts and Actions Through an Exceptional BDI Foundation
A Call to Action

With Dr. Natasha Reyes and Dr. Leonard Steen

As a Psych [psychologist] I remember talking about deficits simply led us nowhere. I remember after creating the PSP [problem-solving process] together and presenting to teams, I heard so many regular education teachers say, "This finally broke the cycle of saying 'here is the problem, here is what we tried, it didn't work . . . here is the problem, here is what we tried, it didn't work.'" When you ask what a person CAN do, you will always get an answer and a starting point, which makes everyone involved feel the progress . . . it's human nature to want to succeed. If we focus on the failures, we will give up, we will not make progress, we will not evolve. But if we ask, "what CAN I do?" the answer will always be positive!

—Denise Walton, Interlocal Assistant Director, Special Education

This chapter focuses on the positive, what we *can* do, but also the imperative to never lose sight of the *why*. A long history exists regarding the nuanced work of meeting the needs of CLD learners, including those being considered for referral, in the referral process, or receiving services, in culturally and linguistically responsive ways. Twenty years into public school service, one of the authors of this text, Dr. Robin Cabral, explored teachers' referral of CLD learners for special education (Cabral, 2008). The context of the study was a large Midwestern district experiencing rapid growth in CLD students, especially those with a home language other than English. This research revealed several commonalities among referring teachers' experiences and precepts teaching CLD students. Among these were the teachers'

1. Self-reported *lack of preparation* to teach CLD students,
2. Tendency to *overrate students' English* proficiencies as "enough English,"
3. *Disregard for language* as relevant to individual students' learning, and
4. *Lack of CLD consideration* during intervention.

Together, these phenomena served to reinforce status quo methods for instruction and identification. In essence, a student's failure with nonaccommodative interventions appeared to validate teacher perceptions of prereferral as simply a *confirmatory* process rather than the means by which learning problems could be resolved. These phenomena were compounded by overall deference to psychological test data (the scores) and preference for special education placement as the "best chance" for *this* student's success.

Findings from the research gained traction within the district's special education leadership just as its newest elementary school, "Los Olmos," opened with freshly assigned staff. It was an optimal opportunity to innovate within parameters of prescribed practice. One potential area of innovation was the district's **general education intervention (GEI)** process. The new building's principal supported reimagining the GEI process as an asset-driven model of discovering "what works" for each student. A brainstorming approach to intervention was considered not just potentially more appropriate for the majority CLD neighborhood, but likely better aligned with the *culturally responsive* and *communication/collaboration* guidance included in the state's model of multitiered systems of support (MTSS). As part of the principal's vision for the school's culture of inclusivity, teachers also learned about biography-driven instruction (Herrera, 2016).

Within three years, Los Olmos's instructional practices, family involvement, and achievement gained notice. More specifically, referrals for special education were lower than at other area schools. In addition to teachers reporting the benefits of asset-driven instruction *for all*, many also experienced professional growth through the BDI-framed discussions around interventions for *the few*. The positive results for Olmos were so compelling that the problem-solving process (PSP) was adopted as the GEI system for the entire district. Systematic rollout emphasized that the design of the PSP was to target those students for whom the "most intensive" supports were indicated. Consistent with response to intervention (RTI) or MTSS, such types of support necessarily fall outside the interventions afforded every student to assure success (Herrera, Cabral, & Murry, 2020; Reyes, 2022).

The guiding PSP form featured identification of student *strengths* that could be drawn upon to develop individualized interventions in any area(s) of concern (e.g., communication, math, writing, reading, behavior). The focus intentionally directed dialogue away from common deficit thinking (enumeration of failures) to embrace an attitude of success through strengths. To serve as a reminder of this purpose, the form included the summative accountability statement, "Problem solving process is complete when the team can describe the conditions under which the student is *successful*."

Among early challenges to implementation of the PSP were comments of veteran staff who regarded the process as mere rebranding of standard practice. Others grasped the expanded detail but declared it impossible to spend more time on individualized discussion of referred students. There were simply too many of them! Occasionally, these discussions led to schoolwide growth via onsite problem solving around rates of referral. Did some grades refer more than others? What types of concerns were cited most often in grades with the highest referrals? How could the team be supported to problem solve around emergent patterns to identify grade-level adaptations to instruction?

Opportunities to explore such conversations proved powerful—*where invited*, but the milieu of the initiative was "invite only." Administrators or child study team (CST) members had to seek additional guidance. As a result, implementation was not monitored and few schools, teams, or administrators requested support. That left the form, with all of its embedded intention, as the primary framework for practice. Those who engaged in deeper reflection with supported application remain invested in transformed practices to this day. One former school psychologist who piloted ideas and contributed to PSP development wrote: "Seriously, the Problem-solving process comes up in so many of my thoughts and my conversations now, it has changed the way I view my job and my world!" Another school psychologist who was an early adopter shared the following:

> The problem-solving process pushed me to look outside of my "professional box" and challenged the way I interpreted information. . . . When looking at a whole child perspective, it allowed for the creation of more specific interventions, increasing the chances of [student] success.

Five years after implementation of PSP as the GEI process used districtwide, old trends persisted, reemerging at sites that had previously reduced referrals. Of note, while referrals and identification of CLD students for special education ticked up, overall district enrollment was decreasing. CLD students qualifying for English for speakers of other languages (ESOL) enrollment had also decreased. These data suggested that despite efforts to address overreferral of CLD students into special education, representation remained disproportional (Reyes, 2022).

Trends were most apparent to personnel assigned to "test" the growing lists of CLD students who were "failing" despite the prescribed tiers of MTSS support. These numbers begged exploration, especially given the decades of studies on **disproportionality** of CLD students in special education (Artiles et al., 2002; Skiba et al., 2008; Sullivan, 2011; Voulgarides, 2018). Of particular interest was the role of referral processes (Cabral, 2008; Coutinho

& Oswald, 2000), specifically those that lacked culturally respectful materials and failed to value the cultural differences of learners (Hoover, 2012). The PSP implemented in this district had emphasized identification of student strengths to facilitate success, with focus on parent and family perspectives, so recent trends necessitated a deeper dive. What was going on (or not going on) with the new process to lessen the power of its initial promise?

Two tenets of BDI (Herrera, 2016) served as a framework for a case study (Reyes & Steen, 2021) to delve into the PSP in this district:

1. The importance of attending to the biopsychosocial histories of students
2. The importance of considering data and sources of knowledge outside of standardized assessments or benchmark screeners to determine levels of development and ability

Given this framework, the study sought to investigate how students' cultural-linguistic diversity was considered in the data collected/analyzed during the GEI process. Researchers also hoped to gain insight into the types of data used to describe CLD students and their school performance in written descriptions of those students' area(s) of need.

Findings from the study revealed a paucity of discussion around students being culturally and/or linguistically diverse. In fact, just over half of the PSP forms analyzed contained no reference to CLD considerations beyond listing students' home language or indicating receipt of ESOL services. This finding was unexpected because data were limited to forms for students determined to be CLD by English as a second language status or a home language other than English. In at least one instance, the need to consider cultural-linguistic diversity was flatly dismissed because the student was being "looked at for strengths and possible enrichment reasons only, [so] ESOL will not necessarily be needed for this process" (Reyes & Steen, 2021). Interestingly, it was typically the speech-language pathologist, when consulted, who referenced students' cultural and linguistic diversity and its possible impact on communication in classroom settings. Other findings indicated a lack of qualitative data, limited information related to student strengths, few descriptions

of the student outside of the academic setting, and a scarcity of actual instructional adjustments made during the PSP. Absence of detail was conspicuous as the process forms were designed specifically to guide conversations for problem solving on individual students' learning, *contextualized* by their lived experience. Overall, analysis of the PSP forms revealed the following:

- Rare mention or consideration of students being culturally and linguistically diverse
- Inadequate/missing description of student strengths
- Lack of information provided from parent/family perspectives
- Overwhelming reliance on quantitative data from universal screenings

There was, in sum, no evidence of participating members' ability or inclination to understand students from a biopsychosocial standpoint or, in other words, from the lens of the "whole child" (Reyes, 2022). Students were, in effect, reduced to the person they appeared to be *at school*.

Though limited in scope, this case study provided a basis to explore district phenomena at a deeper level. Specifically, the researchers hoped to better understand the language used, data deemed important, and perspectives of educators involved in problem-solving for CLD students. To this end, two concurrent studies were undertaken. One focused on perspectives of the referring teachers (Reyes, 2022) while another looked at the practices and mindsets of **child study team (CST)** members supporting the process (Steen, 2022).

EXPLORING PERSPECTIVES OF REFERRING TEACHERS

Although policies, practices, and research have been collectively utilized to address the disproportionate representation of CLD students in special education, most exist within the realm of special education (Bradley et al., 2007). Few studies have explored the factors impacting these issues within general education (Waitoller et al., 2010). To further this research and gain insight on the implementation of PSP, Reyes (2022) explored the participation of general education classroom teachers. Reyes sought to examine the sources referenced and language used by classroom teachers discussing CLD learners in the PSP.

The participants were self-selected classroom teachers familiar with the PSP who reported experience with culturally and linguistically diverse students. Each had either initiated the PSP or taught a student in this process from the prior case study. Data collected were analyzed through a BDI lens, as well as by utilizing Gee's (2011) building task tools for examining how language conveyed *privileged information*, *social goods*, and *beliefs or perspectives*. Overall, the findings from the analysis indicated a "lack of awareness, knowledge, and consideration of the impact of a student's biopsychosocial history within the academic setting" (Reyes, 2022, p. 96). The themes that emerged 14 years after Cabral (2008) reported on recurrent perspectives related to CLD students, the referral process, and data considered important to this process included the following (Reyes, 2022):

1. *The role of parents/families* (assumptions held by the classroom teacher about parents and expected behavior)
2. *Teacher self-perceptions* (the perceived importance of teacher knowledge over, or without, consideration of the family/parent perspective)
3. *Storytelling* (how a student's story was utilized, if at all, within the classroom during consideration for interventions and during interpretation of data)
4. *Misunderstanding of the individual problem-solving process* (mindsets of classroom teachers around "struggling" students and the desire to "hurry up and test")

Despite these trends, some teachers evidenced desires to improve their understanding of factors related to CLD student performance and gain additional knowledge for both instruction and interventions for CLD students. However, teachers commonly misunderstood the PSP. For example, statements such as "you're putting in there different focus points that you're wanting to really focus in on for the student, so that way you can potentially,

hopefully, get them tested for special education" demonstrate a general misunderstanding of the process. This teacher was heavily focused on the end goal of a special education evaluation in contrast to the intended outcome of the process, which is to find success for the student. Despite their misunderstanding, participants also expressed interest in training designed to support them in translating guidelines into practice and increasing students' grade-level achievement on the standards-based curriculum.

When considering the district's GEI process—which was aligned with the MTSS and RTI models and had the potential to reduce inappropriate referrals, decrease inappropriate identification for special education, and inform culturally responsive/respectful instruction (Bagasi, 2014; Enrique et al., 2013; Montalvo et al., 2014; NCRTI, 2010)—an apparent point of disconnect for the teachers was a lack of opportunities to be supported in brainstorming around student assets and needs. In this district, such support was assumed to include the specialized insights of the CST. Therefore, a distinct study of CST roles in referral and placement was concurrently undertaken.

EXAMINING PRACTICES AND PERSPECTIVES OF CHILD STUDY TEAMS

In this district, a CST typically includes a psychologist, speech-language pathologist, counselor, social worker, nurse, and administrator. These teams evaluate students for special education, but they are also involved in intervention processes. They may suggest strategies to support learners (Klingner & Harry, 2006), conduct various screenings, assist in data collection, and help determine when referral for evaluation is appropriate. Steen (2022) explored how one CST team at an elementary school in this district considers language and culture in these processes.

In this school, a CST representative attends each problem-solving discussion to help with data collection and decision-making. Although the current PSP had been implemented for 10 years, there appeared to be continued reliance on universal or generalized interventions during the process, without consideration of students' backgrounds. During problem-solving discussions within grade-level teams, the priority for CST representatives seemed to be ensuring completeness of the process forms (i.e., making sure all numerical data was included and interventions named). As one CST member remarked, "I know I'm being nitpicky, but this is what's coming down on us. So, in order to even say, 'yes, this kid needs an evaluation,' based on what we have right now, the answer would be no" (Steen, 2022).

The intent of this process—to find student success through individualized intervention—was not apparent during these discussions. Instead, emphasis was placed on demonstrating lack of progress to confirm teachers' existing perceptions and achieve timely referral for special education evaluation. If students did not respond to instruction as it was, it was assumed that they must need help. Because instructional strategies and specific interventions were not reevaluated or altered, blame was assigned to students instead of looking at the systems. This type of response has been widely documented (e.g., Hernández Finch, 2012; Kangas, 2021; Matias & Mackey, 2016).

CST members expressed regret that students were not evaluated sooner so they could receive the "support" in special education perceived to be necessary for academic achievement. Had the process been implemented as designed, appropriate instructional support would have been in place either prior to or without referral for special education evaluation. Instead, students were referred when they failed to meet expectations, a finding consistent with existing research (Garcia & Ortiz, 2006; Hoover, 2012). Regardless of the results of this process and reasons for referrals, both seemed to be disregarded once students entered the evaluation process. Upon referral "signoff," evaluations were conducted with a general lack of consideration for quality or sources of data. There was little to no evidence of assessment planning as required by IDEA (Sec. 300.304). Such planning is necessary to ensure that the areas and means of assessment are appropriate to inform understanding of the specific concerns noted by teachers and parents. How else can a team develop, where indicated, an appropriate IEP?

Instead, there was an apparent reliance on English-language *standardized testing*, where scores are obtained from administration of assessments using scripted procedures. Scores so obtained seemed to be the primary or even sole determinant for special education eligibility and need. This finding was consistent with previous studies (e.g., Hoover et al., 2018; Orosco & Klingner, 2010) that have found similar dependence on English-language standardized assessment, including the study conducted by Cabral 14 years earlier (Cabral, 2008). Sometimes, these scores were accompanied by warnings that they "may under-represent students' abilities," yet they were still used to make concrete statements describing cognitive functioning (e.g., that a student functions "in the very low range cognitively"). Absent consideration for students' backgrounds, performance was reduced to individual capacities or effort without consideration for factors outside of the assessments; recommended practices, such as triangulation of data, use of alternate measurements/information, and students' biopsychosocial histories (Herrera, Cabral, & Murry, 2020; Rhodes et al., 2005), ultimately were not considered when interpreting results.

Qualitative, biography-driven data from parents (and occasionally school staff) indicated that appropriate abilities were dismissed in favor of standardized assessment, even when contradictory. Students' functional and social language strengths were dismissed as "the difference between social and academic language" to rationalize perceived deficits in language determined through assessment. In this way, belief in the presence of disability was reinforced because of a perceived lack of skills and knowledge assumed requisite for appropriate functioning (i.e., those skills measured by standardized assessment). The insights of parents and families, who are a valuable source of information about students' functioning, knowledge, strengths, and weaknesses (Herrera, Cabral, & Murry, 2020; Marr y Ortega, 2022), were unexplored, dismissed, or underutilized.

Participants rationalized their rejection of parents' input when caregivers did not share the school's concerns (Steen, 2022). Parents were perceived to be uneducated, lacking understanding of their children's educational difficulties, and unable to help with academics, which resulted in the perspective that their information "needs to be taken with a grain of salt." These negative perceptions of students and their parents reinforced persistent assumptions about what knowledge and experiences are valuable or necessary, and characterized the diverse characteristics of students' backgrounds as deficits instead of assets.

In the state in which this study was completed, placement requires documentation of both *eligibility* and *need* for special education. Eligibility is determined through evaluation indicating a potential disability/disorder. Need can only be determined through identifying the supports and instructional strategies necessary for success. Without a well-implemented PSP, the question of *need* cannot be answered.

Failures during these processes result in special education placements for diverse learners that are potentially inappropriate and inadequate for their instructional needs. Research shows that outcomes for students placed in special education are, in fact, not always positive or neutral. Lowered expectations (Aron & Loprest, 2012) and lack of individualized instruction (Harry & Klingner, 2014) can actually result in poorer long-term outcomes than those of general education peers (Aron & Loprest, 2012; Hernández Finch, 2012).

THE ELEPHANT IN THE PROCESS

The parable of the blind men and the elephant is commonly shared across the world. What follows is an adapted version.

> Once, a group of blind men were called upon to help their ruler. She was advised that a strange animal had been brought to the kingdom, and these men were famous for their ability to infer knowledge by touch. They readily agreed to help: "We must inspect this creature to advise the Queen how best to respond." When they came upon an elephant, they each groped part of its outer surface. The first man, whose hand landed on the trunk, said, "This being is like a thick snake." Stroking the broad, flat ear, another declared, "It must be some sort of fan." The next man, whose hand was upon the elephant's leg,

> said, "This animal is a pillar like the trunk of a tree." The man who placed his hand upon its side proclaimed the animal "a mighty wall." Another, who felt its tail, described it laughingly "no more than a simple rope." The last blind man felt its tusk and shouted, "Beware!" for it was "hard and smooth, most likely a spear."

Six different interpretations will unsurprisingly beget six different conclusions. The parable of the elephant and the blind men cautions us to avoid interpretation of findings from limited perspectives, regardless of expertise. Decontextualized observations easily lead to faulty conclusions and misguided responses. Reliance on measuring and inferring from "parts" contributes to misidentification of the "whole." In what ways does the story of the blind men parallel findings from the studies highlighted in this chapter? How do our structures and language around measures of isolated tasks reinforce the same sort of tendencies that led the men to proclaim the elephant a wall, a spear, or merely a rope? Do the processes and language used in schools foster insight into the interconnectedness of parts, held together by unmeasured strengths? Is it possible that a hyperfocus on *select* indicators (e.g., tail, leg) may cause us to overlook the individual's highly communicative eyes? In this sense, it is less physical blindness that obscures perception than blinders of mindsets and language.

Sara Kangas (2021) reminds us that CLD students' *needs* are frequently framed in terms of *language* or *disability*. Efforts to avoid the misidentifications that contribute to disproportionality encourage a distinction between language and disability as the primary cause of low achievement. Such language both sets up and perpetuates mindsets that learning problems are always student-held. As Kangas (2021) notes, one never hears forced determination that giftedness or scholarly accomplishment is due to language or (dis)ability. False dichotomies and frameworks that evaluate only the *student* undermine opportunities for *systemic* reflection and growth. More significantly, the data we value and the ways we talk about students can perpetuate the mindsets that factor in disproportional representation of CLD students in special education.

Other ways data resemble the decontextualized perceptions of the blind men from our story include these:

- Use of cutoff scores from marketed screeners to "group" students (e.g., RTI tiers)
- Reliance on similarly constructed probes to gauge (unaccommodated) learning
- CST members' evaluation and presentation of skills by discrete area (speech, social, cognitive, etc.)
- Description of skills on IEPs (present levels and goals) devoid of insight on how the skills are demonstrated across settings and languages

Clearly, all the required and monitored components of referral, placement, and service matter, but how often have the assurances provided in IDEA become the benchmark indicators in and of themselves? When viewed as independently valid indicators (e.g., parent attendance at meeting = parent involvement), markers of accountability can be reduced to check boxes. Did it occur? Yes or no. When addressed in this way, the purpose of assuring parental involvement is entirely lost.

Voulgarides (2018) writes,

> the social context and organizational contexts of schools and districts, coupled with color blind and race-neutral approaches to education, allow for educators to treat compliance as a means to an end, rather than opportunity to question how people, policies, and educational practices can be aligned to achieve equity in special education. (p. 102)

Emphasis on compliance as checked boxes precludes the spirit and intent of the process. We not only lose the benefits of community building practices, but we also lose the power of each assurance to impact the very reasons we require compliance.

Losing sight of the *why* blinds us to the need for developing and applying the growth mindset intended by the law. School systems frequently find themselves "engulfed in a compliance paradigm which does not provide space for educators to sufficiently consider the effects that social context and their own personal and professional capacities have on educational practice when using educational policy" (Voulgarides, p. 105). This chapter encourages readers to critically reflect: *What can we do collectively to chart a new path forward?*

There are no easy answers, and every educator has a role to play. When the *how* of our work remains true to the *why*, our processes reflect the advocacy at the heart of laws designed to ensure full educational access to *all* students. When the process is truly equitable, a CLD student who is eligible and in need of special education support is participating in classes and instruction that maximize learning, language, and social opportunities. Figure 8.1 summarizes what IDEA says, why particular pieces were included, and how we can ensure lawful and effective practice with CLD learners. Figure 8.2 (and the related tool in Appendix B) can be used to support the process of developing IEP goals that are responsive to the learner's multidimensional biographical assets. As we bring this book to a close, we urge readers to keep in mind the *whole*—the whole reason we have assurances to protect individual students' rights, the whole student in the context of their family and community, and opportunities for learners to participate in school as equal members of a whole, inclusive classroom community.

Figure 8.1. Alignment of IDEA and BDI

A BDI Perspective on the *What, Why,* and *How* of IDEA

WHAT . . . does IDEA say?	WHY . . . was it included?	HOW . . . do we ensure lawful practice with CLD students?
Takeaways From Key Definitions		
Native Language—when used with respect to an individual who is Limited English Proficient, the language normally used by the individual, or in the case of a child, the language normally used by the parents	Students must be able to use and access their primary language(s) to *validly* demonstrate knowledge that is stored, conceptualized, or better expressed through that language or language *system*. Otherwise, we are not measuring the student's true abilities or skills, which is necessary to determine disability.	For ethical compliance, teams and evaluators regard *language* as an interactive system within bilingually exposed students. Bilingualism can be likened to the ways we use two hands together for tasks regardless of handedness or dominance. Adherence to the spirit of IDEA can be demonstrated through observation or elicitation of skills in bilingual contexts (e.g., bilingual evaluator) and/or informed triangulation of assets across contexts and settings.

Specific Learning Disability—a disorder in one or more of the basic psychological processes involved in understanding or in using language, spoken or written, which disorder may manifest in the imperfect ability to listen, think, speak, read, write, spell, or do mathematical calculations. . . . Such term does not include a learning problem that is primarily the result of a visual, hearing, or motor disability, of intellectual disabilities, of emotional disturbance, or of environmental, cultural, or economic disadvantage.	With a specific learning disability, learning problems or skill deficits are innate to the individual child. Therefore, they will be noted to occur in all settings where related processes are needed to interact or perform a task.
	• Anytime a significant component of a student's learning or skill delay is attributable to environmental or situational/external factors,* the student may need accommodations to participate in the grade-level curriculum but does not possess a true disability.
	• *External factors that can impact learning include:
	  » Mobility
	  » Attendance
	  » Trauma
	  » Less effective program models (i.e., English-only instruction, pull-out ESOL)
	  » Lack of access to ESOL supports (waivered)
	  » Lack of appropriate instruction in reading or math
		Avoid negating exclusionary factors (culture, educational experience, language, etc.) as relevant to the child's current success. The term "exclusionary" does not require teams to "rule out" factors contributing, rather it requires the team to exclude them as the *primary* cause of lower achievement. A student does not cease to be bilingual or CLD once they are identified as also having a learning disability.
		• Special education placement adds to, but *does not rewrite*, a student's biography.
		• A robust process is necessary to ensure that student assets and needs have been considered during instruction. Documentation should show how the student's skill or language levels were met in ways that would demonstrate response to (biography-informed) instruction. Use of biography-driven approaches and interventions allows teams greater confidence in statements around the required *appropriateness of instruction*, despite or in conjunction with factors listed in the second column.

Figure 8.1. (*Continued*)

WHAT . . . does IDEA say?	WHY . . . was it included?	HOW . . . do we ensure lawful practice with CLD students?
Transition Services—a coordinated set of activities that focuses on improving the academic and functional achievement of a child with a disability to facilitate movement from school to post-school activities . . . [such as] instruction, related services, community experiences, the development of employment and other post-school adult living objectives	Developmental and functional goals must have long-term relevance for the individual student. • IEP developers are guided to think in terms of incremental development of skills and capacities that will best support the student's pursuit of interests, employment, self-care, and participation within the community.	Key considerations include: • Does the transition plan reflect the skills and communication methods necessary for success within the student's personal, social, and economic community? • Is the ongoing use of home/community language(s) represented among transition outcomes?

Critical Question: How does the information revealed through BDI permit more appropriate consideration of concepts such as native language, transition, and the role of external factors in determining eligibility and planning for the appropriate instruction of CLD students?

Evaluation/Reevaluation
Act, 20 U.S.C. § 1414 (2004)

A variety of assessment tools and strategies should be used, including information provided by parents to determine: • Whether a child has a disability • How best to enable the child to be involved and progress in the general education curriculum	Point-in-time or high-stakes assessments may not yield accurate information. A true disability will be evident across contexts, including within the home environment. Parent information is crucial to such determinations. Information related only to test performance or static skill levels does not inform discussion of the conditions under which the student *does* succeed. Such insights are essential to write an individual education plan that addresses levels of support and accommodations necessary for a specific student to participate in each area of the curriculum, including general education.	Parent information that merely reflects teacher commentary or class expectation (e.g., "his teacher says he doesn't know . . ., can't do . . .") and relates to school is not evidence of difficulties in home settings. Conversely, strengths or needs situated in the home environment (e.g., "needs repeated help . . ., follows directions, communicates needs, retells events") may provide important support or refutation of the difficulties noted at school.

(*Continued*)

Figure 8.1. (*Continued*)

WHAT . . . does IDEA say?	WHY . . . was it included?	HOW . . . do we ensure lawful practice with CLD students?
No single measure or assessment can be the sole criterion for determining disability or educational program.	Any apparent deficit must be pervasive across settings that employ a particular skill or process. If a problem only exists in one setting, task, context, or language, it is unlikely to be innate. Furthermore, single measures and point-in-time assessments are subject to numerous variables related to the person and appropriateness of the test/task.	This area is one of the most overlooked. Upon noticing student weakness with any skill, informed evaluators consider the assumptions inherent to the task used to "measure" that skill. Key considerations include: • What other variables may have affected student performance? • How might we probe that skill in a situation or task where we are able to lessen the impact of language or experience?
Assessments and other evaluation materials used to assess students under this section of IDEA: • Are selected and administered so as not to be discriminatory on a racial or cultural bias • Are provided and administered in the language and form most likely to yield accurate information on what the child knows and can do academically, developmentally, and functionally, unless it is not feasible to do so or administer • Are used for purposes for which the assessments or measures are valid and reliable	The purpose of the evaluation is to determine whether a given student, regardless of experience or opportunity, is also a student with a true disability. Evidence that a student is simply behaving or performing differently from peers is insufficient to resolve questions related to *why*.	Know yourself: • What preconceptions or ideals do I bring to my role as an evaluator? • What do I think is the purpose of assessment and evaluation? Know your role: • Why is my area of insight relevant to understanding a student's lack of success in *current programming*? • What type of data (e.g., scores, descriptions, context analysis) is most informative to the purpose of *this* evaluation? Know your test: • Are students' experiences, language(s), economic opportunities, etc., like those of the *majority* of the population on which this test was normed? • Can I or should I break standardization (e.g., how the test is administered) to gain better insight into *this* student's skills? • Will this test provide insight into this student's fundamental capacities in an area that relates to the *specific* academic concern?

Figure 8.1. (Continued)

WHAT . . . does IDEA say?	WHY . . . was it included?	HOW . . . do we ensure lawful practice with CLD students?
		Know your student: • Why have I selected *this* test and method of administration for *this* student? • Given *this* learner's biography, what accommodations are necessary to reduce barriers to *this* student showing their true abilities? • How will I dynamically probe an area of suspected weakness?

A child shall not be determined to be a child with a disability if the determinant factor for such determination is:
• Lack of appropriate instruction in reading
• Lack of appropriate instruction in math
• Limited English proficiency
	Impediments to learning cannot be largely attributable to external factors.
	
	A child disenfranchised from full participation in the grade-level curriculum due to (1) language proficiency or (2) prior/current opportunity to learn resulting from ineffective instruction may demonstrate achievement deficits. Such students would benefit from informed accommodations but are not students whose needs are attributable to disability.
		Ideally, consideration of instructional appropriateness occurs during development or adoption of the general education curriculum.
		• If more than a small number of students do not demonstrate expected growth, the system should reflect upon:
		  » The appropriateness of literacy approaches/materials for the community of learners
		  » Methods used to assess attainment of skills
		  » Attention to individual student biographies during intervention development
		• Identification of contributing factors, especially related to instruction or assessment, may prompt system changes that lead to improved achievement for all students.

In determining whether a child has a specific learning disability, a local education agency may use a process that determines if the child responds to scientific, research-based intervention as a part of the evaluation. . . .	The local education agency is not compelled to use (potentially limited or flawed) standardized assessments in the determination of specific learning disability.	Familiarize yourself with the research base of the curriculum and methods. Key considerations include: • How do selected methods align with the recommendations put forth in research explicitly focused on CLD students (e.g., August & Shanahan, 2017)? • Do the learning models referenced (e.g., science of reading, biography-driven instruction) negate or potentiate differences in student language, experience, and assets throughout the instructional experience?

(Continued)

Figure 8.1. (*Continued*)

WHAT . . . does IDEA say?	WHY . . . was it included?	HOW . . . do we ensure lawful practice with CLD students?
Reevaluation of student strengths, needs, and program appropriateness shall occur at least once every three years.	Consideration of student skills and functioning, including within the home environment, must reflect the learner's current assets and needs to account for cognitive and linguistic development. Thorough evaluation of the role of language is essential, as linguistic skills develop differently across settings and conditions. Updated information is necessary to assess program appropriateness and plan for continued progress toward the student's transition ideals.	Consideration of a CLD student's fluid language proficiencies, the potential (in)validity of previous assessments, and the dynamic nature of language development compels robust compilation of new insights to student skills and programming. Language(s) of the home and/or student need not be ruled out or "selected" for testing. A BDI lens on assessment allows language to be described in the context of the student's biography, with an emphasis on *access* to instruction as provided.

Critical Question: Have I gathered information that informs *how* a student learns, rather than simply under "what label" or "where" the learning takes place?

Responding to Educational Need

Eligibility and Educational Need: • the determination of whether the child is a child with a disability as defined in section 1401(3) of this title *and* the educational needs of the child shall be made by a team of qualified professionals and the parent of the child	A student may be *eligible* for special education but not have a *need* (e.g., a student with dyslexia who is successful with tiered support). If the student's needs can be met within the range of educational supports and accommodations available to general education students, there is no need for special education.	Consider the whole student. Assuring "need" for special education is an especially critical consideration for CLD learners. Placement in special education may limit access to the instructional methods, accommodations, and settings (with general education peers) that *enhance* language acquisition and its social/educational use.
The Individualized Education Program team must include: • The parents (or guardian) of a child with a disability • Not less than 1 regular education teacher • Not less than 1 special education teacher • A representative of the local education agency who . . . (iv) (ii) is knowledgeable about the general education curriculum.	Representation of parties with knowledge of the student across settings is required to develop a plan for assistance with targeted areas of need while also ensuring maximum access to general education instruction, settings, and peers.	Interpreters trained in special education processes and assurances are necessary to facilitate parents' informed participation in the process of developing their child's IEP. Cultural mediators are essential to ensuring recognition of cultural assets and contextualization of the student within the larger community (see also *Transition Services*). Language support programs such as dual language and ESOL are components of general education to which CLD students remain entitled. IEP development should reflect involvement and inclusion of these personnel to assure continued access with accommodations as necessary for student needs.

Figure 8.1. (*Continued*)

WHAT . . . does IDEA say?	WHY . . . was it included?	HOW . . . do we ensure lawful practice with CLD students?
In developing an IEP, the IEP team should consider: • The strengths of the child • Concerns of the parents for enhancing the education of their child The IEP team must also assure consideration of special factors such as the student's: • Ongoing acquisition of English • Mode of communication (e.g., sign language) • Opportunities for direct communications with peers and professionals in the student's mode of communication • Need for assistive technology	The IEP is written in a manner that acknowledges the student's mode of communication as it relates to English-language development, opportunities to communicate with teachers and peers, and the use of communication devices.	Descriptions of the student's home capacities powerfully inform IEP development. Key considerations include: • How does information on the IEP, or presented in the IEP process, distinguish between existing knowledge and language that is not yet demonstrated in the language or contexts of school (difference), and the skills or processes impacted by disability? • How does our knowledge of student *assets* inform (1) development of the IEP (2) reduction of access barriers in both the general education *and* special education settings? • How does implementation of accommodated or modified BDI strategies during special education service (e.g., class within a class, pull-out) mediate barriers related to types of special education services and materials that further disenfranchise CLD students from language and curricular growth?

Critical Question: How does attention to the student's biography during IEP development assure the individualization necessary to meet the spirit and law inherent to IDEA?

CONCLUSION

The final chapter of this text provided insights to the layers of complexity surrounding intent, processes, and practices that impact the appropriateness of the services offered and provided to CLD students with presumed and actual special education needs. Readers are cautioned that focus on the surface efficiencies of paperwork or processes (e.g., flow charts) may inadvertently derail alignment of policy and practice. This chapter concludes by returning our focus to the *intent* of the laws protecting students with disabilities, manifested in the lives of CLD learners with special education needs. It calls every educator to action beyond the "prescribed formulas" used to make determinations with children who live outside the prescribed mold. Specifically, this book reminds readers of the urgency to take action that moves beyond the question, *Is it language or disability?*

As the first part of this book documents, we have lived in the "coal mine" for too long. There is much more that encompasses the culturally and linguistically diverse learner. Shifting our focus from this question allows us as educators to let go of long-held beliefs that may have located problems within CLD learners. A deficit point of view keeps us from seeing the learner's potential and the assets that are culturally, linguistically, and cognitively bound. Instruction that allows students to make public what they know is critical to fully documenting how each learner processes and makes use of information.

Figure 8.2. Biography-Driven Goal Development Tool

Skill to be demonstrated:

When might this skill or behavior naturally occur in the following settings?

- School: _____

    _____

- Home: _____

    _____

Which strategy will create opportunities for *this* student to observe, attempt, revise, and practice this skill?

How might I observe or expand skill development/use during the following conditions?

- i (individual student): _____

    _____

- T (total group): _____

    _____

- p (pairs/partners):

    _____

    _____

- s (small groups): _____

    _____

- I (individual accountability): What will goal attainment look like for this student? _____

    _____

Throughout this book, we encouraged the reader to reimagine what is possible by planning for and setting conditions that are asset-driven. In such contexts our exploration begins with strength-based/asset-driven instruction that provides multiple points of entry for all learners. Creating this type of ecology requires framing our instruction through a biography-driven lens, in which we recognize that every learner has something to contribute, and where the product will highlight what is known and what still must be facilitated and navigated by the teacher. It is only through our instruction that we can situationally assess what learners have produced and what cognitive processes they have used to arrive at the destination. In biography-driven classrooms, we observe for and respond to the languages and skills that students use not only by systematically and consistently allowing authentic academic conversations to occur, but also by employing situational awareness and providing tools to scaffold learners' success. Such tools move beyond merely providing a Venn diagram or a worksheet and instead offer personalized avenues for documenting and monitoring learning as it evolves.

Ultimately, although we as authors called out the challenges and caveats to implementing guidelines for CLD learners being considered for referral, in the referral process, or receiving services, our goal was to offer a roadmap for consideration. The last part of this book provided the reader with considerations to guide and support the conversation toward identifying what works, and under what conditions, to ensure that each learner is provided equitable access to assessment and pathways to learning. In this chapter, the metaphor of the blind men and the elephant was used to describe how students often are seen through a narrow system view that has the potential of both limiting our ability to see the brilliance and power that the learner brings from home and community, and defining how students engage, process, and learn in contexts that often are foreign to who they are and what they bring. Our daily pedagogical decisions are influenced by the conclusions we draw about learners. What and how we measure and the actions we take have a lifelong impact on students' lives. From where we stand as educators, administrators, and researchers, our dream is that every child receives the education that is their human right based on systems that no longer revolve around the *language or disability* question but instead ask, *Under what conditions can each learner best shine?*

CHAPTER 8 QUESTIONS FOR REFLECTION AND DISCUSSION

As educators, the first step toward undoing, rethinking, and reimagining is to reflect upon the three C's—challenges, caveats, and considerations—that impact our practices. As professionals in a field that has so many competing agendas, it is critical to reflect upon about our views and perspectives and the role we play in making a difference in the lives of students and families. Reflect on this chapter and independently or collectively with a team, take a position on how you would respond to the following questions.

Challenges

1. What types of assumptions influence the interpretation of data used to identify students at risk in your school?
2. How are these assumptions potentially carried forth and reinforced through patterns of special education referral and placement?

Caveats

1. How would you respond to the statement that all students benefit from special education?
2. How might measures designed to proactively respond to student needs inadvertently result in reducing those students' access to language-rich interactions with teachers and peers?

Considerations

1. What aspects of the research described in Chapter 8 have relevance to your current situation?
2. How does knowledge of IDEA strengthen your capacities and resolve to advocate for CLD students in special education?

Glossary

"ableist": A term used to describe social constructs, attitudes, and language that reflect a presumption that characteristics or abilities considered typical are the ideal. Inherent to ableism are views and practices that focus attention on the need to define and "fix" deficits of persons with differences and disabilities (see also *social model of disability* and *medical model of disability*).

academic dimension: One of the four dimensions of the culturally and linguistically diverse (CLD) student biography. Includes facets of the student's received curriculum and instruction from prekindergarten to high school classrooms and throughout higher education pursuits. Essential to this dimension are factors related to the individual's opportunities for access, engagement, and hope; these can be more difficult to uncover, but they often hold the key to understanding student reactions, given current curriculum, instruction, and academic policy.

activation phase: Taking place during the opening of a lesson, this phase of teaching and learning provides the culturally responsive teacher with opportunities to actively engage students in the new lesson. Teachers observe and document students' connections between the lesson concepts and vocabulary and their background knowledge, which might be drawn from home, community, and/or previous schooling experiences.

affirmation phase: Taking place during the closing of the lesson, this phase of teaching and learning provides the teacher with opportunities to use evidence of student understanding and progress to acknowledge learning. Recognizing the value of both student progress and product, the teacher celebrates growth as well as mastery. The teacher also uses evidence of students' individual cognitive processes to address remaining gaps in understanding.

articulation: This term refers to the place, manner, and precision of speakers when producing oral sounds. Students on an individualized education program for articulation may require support refining production of specific sounds, such as /r/ or /s/ or /l/, that are not language dependent. Students needing articulation support through speech therapy in school will demonstrate errors with articulation in both/all spoken languages.

authentic **cariño***:* A concept that originated in the work of Dr. Angela Valenzuela (1999) and is used to characterize care for learners that includes love and beyond. The term encompasses sharing in learners' joys and struggles, collaborating to ensure everyone succeeds, and developing relationships of trust with families and community members.

biography-driven instruction (BDI): A research-based instructional framework that captures how the four interrelated dimensions of the culturally and linguistically diverse (CLD) student biography, situated within the context of the learner's biopsychosocial history, influence and are continually influenced by the teaching and learning dynamics of the classroom. BDI applies the principles of cultural responsiveness (Gay, 2018) and cultural sustainability (Paris, 2012) to achieve the goals of liberatory praxis as a result of this humanistic, learner-centered, and adaptable approach to teaching and learning in diverse spaces.

biopsychosocial history: A term used to refer to the biological, psychological, and sociological aspects of an individual's background.

Child Find: An essential principle of the Individuals With Disabilities Education Act (IDEA) that requires each school district to identify students who might need special education services in order to ensure access to publicly funded services.

child study team: A school-, district-, or educational cooperative–based team that typically includes a psychologist, speech-language pathologist, counselor, social worker, nurse, and administrator. These teams evaluate students for special education, but they are also involved in intervention processes.

clarification: Communication support that occurs naturally when communicative partners sense a potential breakdown or misunderstanding of a message. Forms of clarification can include listener restatement and requests for repetition or greater specificity of meaning, content, context, or intention behind the message. Speakers engage in clarification by checking for understanding and adding to or refining a message in response to the listener's verbal or nonverbal response. The need to clarify increases as contextual clues and shared understandings decrease.

cognitive dimension: One of the four dimensions of the culturally and linguistically diverse (CLD) student biography. Includes what the students know, how they make sense of new information, and how they apply learning in personally meaningful ways. This dimension also highlights the student's background knowledge (including assets and understandings acquired in the home, community, and school). Highly related to the sociocultural dimension.

connection phase: Taking place during the work time of the lesson, this phase of teaching and learning allows teachers to support students in navigating the curriculum in order to construct meaning. The educator confirms/disconfirms students' understandings and revoices connections made so that individual students' words, ideas, and experiences serve as a gateway to new learning by the entire classroom community. Throughout this phase, the teacher systematically uses intentional grouping structures and configurations to support students as they work collectively, collaboratively, and individually with the new content and language to develop refined understandings.

curb cut effect: A term drawn from studies citing the preferred use of curb cuts on sidewalks by persons physically able to step up a curb. More broadly, this term describes how addressing the disadvantages or exclusions of one group of people creates an environment that enables everyone to participate more easily in that setting.

deficit perspective: A mindset that focuses on students' needs and limitations rather than on their sociocultural, linguistic, cognitive, and academic strengths and assets. This mindset perpetuates an attitude of hopelessness in regard to both the teacher's ability to provide effective accommodations and the student's ability to reach their academic potential.

disproportionality: The degree to which student representation by gender, race, ethnicity, or language learner status does not correlate with those students' representation in the educational setting. This term is often used to describe situations where students of a particular demographic are either under- or overrepresented in a category such as special education.

free and appropriate public education (FAPE): The entitlement of each eligible child with a disability to receive individually designed special education and related services at no cost in the least restrictive environment.

general education intervention (GEI): This term refers to interventions provided to learners in the general education setting. Prior to referral for a special education evaluation, districts must have engaged some form of GEI process, which provides targeted support to students matching their level of need, along with continuous monitoring of progress.

i+Tpsl: An instructional technique that supports educators to systematically and situationally plan and implement grouping structures/

configurations based on the task, students' biographies and socioemotional states of mind, and the planned learning outcomes for the lesson. The mnemonic reminds teachers of the importance of activating the knowledge of the individual learner ("i"), fostering connections and understanding through teacher-directed, text-driven, total-group ("T") work, pairs/ partners ("p") work, and small-teams ("s") work, and providing opportunities for individual accountability ("I") that validate, encourage, and affirm.

Individuals With Disabilities Education Act (IDEA): A law first enacted by Congress in 1975 to ensure that all children with disabilities in the United States and U.S. territories have the opportunity to receive a free and appropriate public education. The law was most recently amended in 2004, with significant additions to and refinement of regulations since that time.

individualized education program (IEP): A child-specific document developed by team members (including parents/guardians) with expertise related to that student and their health, socialization, language, and learning processes. All children in special education are required to have an IEP that is current and accurately reflects their strengths, needs, and the manner in which they will be best supported to meet specified educational goals.

information gap activities: Any type of activity (e.g., barrier games) that promotes the use of descriptive language and clarifying skills under intentionally designed conditions that involve missing information.

instructional conversations (IC): Conversations between the teacher and students that have a didactic purpose and reflect reciprocal and equitable patterns of interaction. During orchestration of an instructional conversation, the teacher skillfully integrates curricular concepts and skills, students' background knowledge and experiences, the utterances of individual learners as they express thought processes and use new language structures, and the emerging ideas of the learning community (Goldenberg, 1992–1993; Herrera, 2022; Holmes, 2022).

joint productive activity (JPA): One of the five Standards for Effective Pedagogy and Learning (CREDE, 2022). Joint productive activity (JPA) involves the teacher and students collaborating together to produce jointly created products. The teacher facilitates, monitors, and supports as students work with peers to develop the activity-related product. A tool in the hand ensures that all learners have the scaffolding they need to engage as equal members of the learning community (Herrera, 2022).

least restrictive environment (LRE): The program or setting in which students are provided the type of supports necessary to maximally participate in, while also being challenged by, the curriculum.

lexicon: The set of words that comprise the vocabulary of a person, group (e.g., age range, region), language, or area of knowledge. For example, the word "shingles" typically means something different in the lexicons of roofers and of doctors, although individuals belonging to either group could have reason to know both meanings.

linguistic dimension: One of the four dimensions of the culturally and linguistically diverse (CLD) student biography. Includes the learner's proficiency in the first and second languages (and any additional languages) and highlights their capacity to comprehend, communicate, and express in each language.

medical model of disability: A lens that views and addresses disability as person-held defects. In the medical model, disability is ascribed to states, traits, and characteristics that differ from what is considered "normal." Differences are regarded as deficits to be cured, fixed, or eliminated in order for the individual to have a more "normal" life.

metalinguistic awareness: The ability to consciously reflect on the structure and form of language, including differences and similarities between languages.

modeling: A form of language facilitation that occurs during genuine interaction and differs from imitation. Effective modeling involves frequent use of a word or sentence pattern while conversing about or explaining something of interest to the listener.

multiple means of engagement: This principle of Universal Design for Learning (UDL) invites teachers to motivate learners in diverse ways, such as those related to interests, personal relevance, or incorporation into preferred activities.

multiple means of expression: This principle of Universal Design for Learning (UDL) encourages teachers to offer students diverse ways of expressing what they have learned. Examples include verbalization, demonstration, art, choice selection, drama, and written products.

multiple means of representation: This principle of Universal Design for Learning (UDL) invites teachers to consider more than one way to explain a concept or provide information. Sensory preferences and object or experience familiarity frequently inform the selection of methods and modes of representation.

multitiered systems of support (MTSS): A comprehensive, proactive system of educational supports implemented throughout a school, district, or educational cooperative. Tiers of support are developed to address academic as well as nonacademic areas (e.g., socioemotional development and behavior) or system goals (e.g., professional development, learning culture, and parent involvement) identified to have an impact on student achievement and educational climate.

nondiscriminatory evaluation: This principle of the Individuals With Disabilities Education Act (IDEA) mandates that measures used to determine eligibility and need in any area of special education be culturally and linguistically nondiscriminatory.

parent participation: A requirement under the Individuals With Disabilities Education Act (IDEA) designed to ensure that parents and guardians are fully informed, and their insights considered, throughout every stage of referral, assessment, placement, and development of an individualized education program (IEP) for special education.

phonology: The sound system of a language, comprised of sounds that can make meaning differences in the words of a specific language.

Phonology includes the rules that govern sound usage in a language. For example, the /ng/ sound is common in English; however, it never occurs at the beginning of an English word. Phonological speech disorders differ from interference between first-language (L1) and second-language (L2) phonologies (sometimes referred to as dialectal variation or accent). A student on an individualized education program (IEP) for phonology may demonstrate error patterns (e.g., omitting sounds and syllables) differently by language, but each will stand out from the production of language peers.

present level of academic achievement and functional performance (PLAAFP): Statements included in an individualized education program (IEP) that describe a student's assets and needs related to progress in general education. Appropriately developed PLAAFPs provide baseline information and coherent connection to the individualized goals and/or services specified for the student.

procedural safeguards: This principle of the Individuals With Disabilities Education Act (IDEA) ensures that the rights of students with disabilities and their parents are afforded protections related to special education processes, documentation, and confidentiality whenever students are considered for, placed in, or receiving special education services.

related services: Any of a number of support services needed by a child with a disability to benefit from special education. Related services include speech-language pathology and audiology services, interpreting services, psychological services, physical and occupational therapy, counseling services, orientation and mobility services, school-based health services, social work services, and transportation.

response to intervention (RTI): A protocol of actions in which schools use data to identify students at risk for poor learning outcomes, monitor student progress or "response," and provide evidence-based interventions to adjust the nature and intensity of supports.

revoicing: The teacher's act of rerouting, expanding upon, or validating students' responses in order to advance the learning of individual students as well as the learning of the larger community of learners.

scaffolding: A variety of tools, strategies, and techniques used by the teacher to support the student's progression to a deeper understanding of concepts while simultaneously building their capabilities to become a more independent learner. Scaffolding provides learners with (1) a conventionalized, ritual *structure* that is both constant and flexible and (2) an interactional *process* that is jointly constructed from moment to moment (van Lier, 2004; Walqui & van Lier, 2010).

social model of disability: In this model, disability is not fully ascribed to the individual but occurs as a result of barriers created by impediments to access designed around community norms.

sociocultural dimension: One of the four dimensions of the culturally and linguistically diverse (CLD) student biography. Includes the students' social and cultural variables, which influence how they navigate academic successes. This dimension is critical to understanding the whole student and how the other three dimensions work. Considered the "heart" of the student biography.

third space: Classroom conditions that reflect responsiveness to the contributions of individual learners and the voice of the collective learning community. The teacher engages in the sense-making process with students. Together, they jointly negotiate discourse and knowledge, utilizing all linguistic and cultural repertoires of practice. Third space is an indicator of culturally relevant, responsive, and sustaining classrooms.

translanguaging: The dynamic and creative use of one's entire linguistic repertoire to make meaning and engage with others.

Universal Design for Learning (UDL): A teaching approach designed around the need to remove or reduce barriers to student learning. Universal Design for Learning promotes flexible practices to enhance the individual student's engagement, expression, and representation of knowledge in learning contexts.

zone of proximal development (ZPD): Vygotsky's (1978) theoretical construct that depicts the space between what a student is independently capable of achieving and the level of achievement possible with the help of peers. When concepts fall within this space, or zone, new learning is most likely to occur. The zone continually shifts as the student grasps new concepts and works with them independently, rather than needing support from the teacher or peers.

Overview of Select BDI Strategies

Note: The strategy descriptions included in this table provide a broad stroke overview of key instructional processes for many strategies discussed in this text. For a full description of each strategy and to explore additional BDI strategies, refer to Herrera et al. (2011) and Herrera et al. (2017).

BDI Strategy Name	Strategy Description
DOTS (Determine, Observe, Talk, Summarize) Chart	The DOTS strategy is designed to activate, connect, and affirm the learner's background knowledge by creating an opportunity to: (1) Determine what they know about the topic/concept(s), (2) use their selective attention to Observe and assess their learning, (3) talk to their peers while utilizing the words and ideas they have documented in their notes, and (4) use the tool to Summarize/Solve in writing during post-instructional assessment. The DOTS Chart tool in the hand is used throughout the lesson as a scaffold not only to guide the student's learning but also to support the teacher's differentiation of instruction.
Extension Wheel	The Extension Wheel strategy supports the learner to identify and organize the key concepts that are necessary to engage in conversations, quick-writes, and post-instructional tasks that require them to extend and apply what was learned. To activate prior knowledge, the teacher asks students to think about the topic/main idea that is going to be covered. As the lesson moves into text, students are asked to make connections to what they know about the topic. The teacher begins to route/guide the learner to the critical knowledge they need to have about the topic, including relationships among concepts and ideas. This provides the teacher an opportunity to have students refer back to what they know, as well as revisit any misconceptions they may have held about the topic. At the end of the lesson, the Extension Wheel provides the learner a source of information to share what they learned. For the teacher, the Extension Wheel supports assessment of how the learner processed the content during the lesson.
Hearts	The Hearts strategy is an inductive way of taking the learner from the known to the unknown. It is often used for topics that evoke an emotional response. Hearts activates students' prior knowledge and experiences by using a three-tier inductive process that leads the student to explain/describe a personally meaningful event or experience related the topic. First, the learner is asked to think of words that come to mind related to the topic. For example, How might someone feel if they experienced a natural disaster (e.g., tornado, flood, earthquake) and lost everything? During the connection phase, the learner moves into text/lecture and writes/draws about natural disasters covered during the lesson. Often the teacher will refer to what the students wrote initially and begin to weave in stories of the natural disasters they have experienced. At the end of the lesson, the teacher guides the student to use their experiences and what they have written on the tool in the hand to compare what was in the text and their own lived reality.

BDI Strategy Name	Strategy Description
Linking Language	Linking Language is a strategy that uses visuals to introduce key vocabulary/concept(s) by providing a canvas of opportunity to inductively bridge from the known the unknown. The teacher selects three or four pictures that illustrate key concepts from the lesson. The students are then divided into groups of four or five students. Learners are asked to draw or write everything they think of or feel when they look at the pictures placed in the center of poster paper. The teacher bridges from students' background knowledge, guiding learners toward deeper understanding of the vocabulary/concepts. The posters are used as anchor charts to refer to as the teacher supports connections between students' words and ideas and the text. Students engage in conversation throughout the lesson and return to the posters to add new ideas. The anchor charts serve as scaffolds for learners as they write or complete post-instructional activities.
Story Bag	The Story Bag is a strategy that supports learners to rehearse essential content vocabulary, while at the same time building critical conceptual knowledge related to the topic. During the activation stage the learner is asked to predict which images/vocabulary words may appear in the text, based on the cover of the story or the topic of the text. As the teacher moves to the connection (text) phase of the lesson, learners are guided to confirm or disconfirm their predictions. Learners explore how the words convey meaning and the teacher facilitates the flow of ideas by lifting and maximizing student voices. Students decide which images/vocabulary words to keep in the bag and what to discard, which provides the teacher the opportunity to take language to the i+1 and each student to their zone of proximal development as the teacher assesses learning in real time. At the end of the lesson, the words confirmed to be in the text are used to summarize what was learned.
U-C-ME (Uncover, Concentrate, Monitor, Evaluate)	The U-C-ME strategy guides the learner in Uncovering and making public their background knowledge related to the topic. The teacher then provides the guiding questions and asks learners to Concentrate and work with their peers in answering the question as the lesson unfolds. By setting the conditions that guide students to draw from the text and their peers as the questions are answered, learners are supported to become strategic and resourceful independent learners as they Monitor their responses. At the end of the lesson the learner is challenged to Evaluate their learning.
Vocabulary Quilt	The Vocabulary Quilt is a strategy that moves teachers beyond the traditional use of word walls by creating a tool in the hand that is student owned. At the beginning of the lesson the quilt serves to draw attention to the eight core vocabulary words. Words on the quilt are selected for their strength in providing students the language necessary to respond to conceptual/comprehension questions related to the topic or reading. The quilt is produced independently or in a small team and allows learners to first activate and document their background knowledge related to the words. The vocabulary words are then defined as the lesson unfolds and the words are encountered in text, with students using both traditional approaches (glossary/dictionary/text) and people resources (teacher/peers). Learners use sticky notes to elaborate or refine meanings of words and then add them to the quilt. At the end of the lesson the quilt is used to scaffold the completion of end-of-lesson assignments.

Template for Biography-Driven Goal Development Tool

BIOGRAPHY-DRIVEN GOAL DEVELOPMENT TOOL

Skill to be demonstrated: _____

When might this skill or behavior naturally occur in the following settings?

- School: _____

  _____

  _____

- Home: _____

  _____

  _____

Which strategy will create opportunities for *this* student to observe, attempt, revise, and practice this skill?
_____

How might I observe or expand skill development/use during the following conditions?

- i (individual student): _____

  _____

  _____

- T (total group): _____

  _____

  _____

- p (pairs/partners): _____

  _____

  _____

- s (small groups): _____

  _____

  _____

- I (individual accountability): What will goal attainment look like for this student? _____

  _____

  _____

References

Alim, H. S., & Paris, D. (2017). What is culturally sustaining pedagogy and why does it matter? In D. Paris & H. S. Alim (Eds.), *Culturally sustaining pedagogies: Teaching and learning for justice in a changing world* (pp. 1–21). Teachers College Press.

Anderson, V., & Roit, M. (1996). Linking reading comprehension instruction to language development for language-minority students. *The Elementary School Journal, 96*(3), 295–309. https://doi.org/10.1086/461829

Aron, L., & Loprest, P. (2012). Disability and the education system. *The Future of Children, 22*(1), 97–122. https://www.jstor.org/stable/41475648

Artiles, A. J. (2022). Interdisciplinary notes on the dual nature of disability: Disrupting ideology–ontology circuits in racial disparities research. *Literacy Research: Theory, Method, and Practice, 71*(1). https://doi.org/10.1177/23813377221120106

Artiles, A. J., Harry, B., Reschly, D. J., & Chinn, P. C. (2002). Over-identification of students of color in special education: A critical overview. *Multicultural Perspectives, 4*(1), 3–10. https://doi.org/10.1207/S15327892MCP0401_2

Artiles, A. J., & Ortiz, A. (2002). *English language learners with special education needs: Identification, assessment, and instruction.* Center for Applied Linguistics. https://eric.ed.gov/?id=ED482995

Artiles, A. J., Rueda, R., Salazar, J., & Higareda, I. (2005). Within-group diversity in minority disproportionate representation: English language learners in urban school districts. *Exceptional Children, 71,* 283–300. https://doi.org/10.1177/001440290507100305

August, D., & Shanahan, T. (2017). *Developing literacy in second-language learners: Report of the National Literacy Panel on Language-Minority Children and Youth.* Routledge.

Baca, L., & Amato, C. (1989). Bilingual special education: Training issues. *Exceptional Children, 56*(2), 168. https://doi.org/10.1177/001440298905600209

Baca, L., & Cervantes, H. (2004). *The bilingual special education interface* (4th ed.). Merrill.

Baca, L., & Cervantes, H. T. (1991). Bilingual special education. *ERIC Digest* E496. https://files.eric.ed.gov/fulltext/ED333618.pdf

Bagasi, M. (2014). *Meta-analysis of the effectiveness of response to intervention models in special education and implications for international implementations* (Publication No. 1557599) [Doctoral dissertation]) ProQuest Dissertations Publishing.

Banerjee, R., & Luckner, J. (2014). Training needs of early childhood professionals who work with children and families who are culturally and linguistically diverse. *Infants & Young Children, 27*(1), 43–59. https://doi.org/10.1097/IYC.0000000000000000

Bartolomé, L. I. (2008). Authentic cariño and respect in minority education: The political and ideological dimensions of love. *International Journal of Critical Pedagogy, 1*(1). http://faculty.www.umb.edu/lilia_bartolome/documents/AuthenticCarinoarticle.pdf

Bhabha, H. (1994). *The location of culture.* Routledge.

Bor, D. (2012). *The ravenous brain: How the new science of consciousness explains our insatiable search for meaning.* Basic Books.

Bradley, R., Danielson, L., & Doolittle, J. (2007). Responsiveness to intervention: 1997–2007. *Teaching Exceptional Children, 39*(5), 8–12. https://doi.org/10.1177/004005990703900502

Bryk, A. S., & Schneider, B. (2002). *Trust in schools: A core resource for improvement.* Russell Sage Foundation.

Cabral, R. M. (2008). *Student learning behaviors and intervention practices cited among Midwestern teachers referring bilingual CLD students for special education evaluation* [Doctoral dissertation, Kansas State University]. K-State Research Exchange. http://hdl.handle.net/2097/932

Casas, C., & Portillo, P. (2000). *Language learning everywhere we go.* Academic Communication Associates.

Center for Research on Education, Diversity & Excellence (CREDE). (2022). *The CREDE five standards for effective pedagogy and learning.* https://manoa.hawaii.edu/coe/credenational/the-crede-five-standards-for-effective-pedagogy-and-learning/

Chamot, A., & O'Malley, J. M. (1994). *The CALLA handbook: Implementing the cognitive academic language learning approach.* Addison-Wesley.

Chick, M. (2014). *The potential of dialogic interaction as a tool for mediating learning during pre-service English language teacher preparation* (Publication No. 27707077) [Doctoral dissertation, University of South Wales]. ProQuest Dissertations Publishing.

Cleave, P. L., Kay-Raining Bird, E., Trudeau, N., & Sutton, A. (2014). Syntactic bootstrapping in children with Down syndrome: The impact of bilingualism. *Journal of Communication Disorders, 49,* 42–54. https://doi.org/10.1016/j.jcomdis.2014.02.006

Coutinho, M. J., & Oswald, D. P. (2000). Disproportionate representation in special education: A synthesis and recommendations. *Journal of Child and Family Studies, 9*(2), 135–156. https://doi.org/10.1023/A:1009462820157

Darling-Hammond, L., Flook, L., Cook-Harvey, C., Barron, B., & Osher, D. (2020). Implications for educational practice of the science of learning and development. *Applied Developmental Science, 24*(2), 97–140. https://doi.org/10.1080/10888691.2018.1537791

Davis, B. M. (Ed.). (2012). *How to teach students who don't look like you: Culturally relevant teaching strategies* (2nd ed.). Corwin Press.

De Valenzuela, J. S., Copeland, S. R., Qi, C. H., & Park, M. (2006). Examining educational equity: Revisiting the disproportionate representation of minority students in special education. *Exceptional Children, 72*(44), 425–441. https://doi.org/10.1177/001440290607200403

Doyle, T. (2011). *Learner-centered teaching: Putting the research on learning into practice.* Stylus Publishing.

Engel, G. (1977). The need for a new medical model: A challenge to biomedicine. *Science, 196*(4286), 129–136.

Enrique, J. A., Adams, K. A., Brockmeier, L. L., & Hilgert, L. D. (April 2013). A preliminary study of disproportionate representation and response to intervention. *Georgia Educational Researcher, 10*(1), 19–33.

Escamilla, K., Hopewell, S., Butvilofsky, S., Sparrow, W., Soltero-González, L., Ruiz-Figueroa, O., & Escamilla, M. (2013). *Biliteracy from the start: Literacy squared in action.* Caslon.

Fabiano-Smith, L., & Goldstein, B. A. (2010). Phonological acquisition in bilingual Spanish-English speaking children. *Journal of Speech, Language, and Hearing Research, 53*(1), 160–178. https://doi.org/10.1044/1092-4388(2009/07-0064)

Ford, D. Y. (2012). Culturally different students in special education: Looking backward to move forward. *Exceptional Children, 78*(4), 391–405. https://journals.sagepub.com/doi/epdf/10.1177/001440291207800401

Frey, J. R. (2019). Assessment for special education: Diagnosis and placement. *The ANNALS of the American Academy of Political and Social Science, 683*(1), 149–161. https://doi.org/10.1177/0002716219841352

Fritzgerald, A. (2020). *Antiracism and universal design for learning: Building expressways to success.* CAST Professional Publishing.

García, O. (2017). Translanguaging in schools: Subiendo y bajando, bajando y subiendo as afterword. *Journal of Language, Identity & Education, 16*(4), 256–263. https://doi.org/10.1080/15348458.2017.1329657

García, S. B., & Ortiz, A. A. (2006). Preventing disproportionate representation: Culturally and linguistically responsive prereferral interventions. *Teaching Exceptional Children, 38*(4), 64–68. https://doi.org/10.1177/004005990603800410

Gates, M. L., & Hutchinson, K. (2005). *Cultural competence education and the need to reject cultural neutrality: The importance of what we teach and do not teach about culture* [Paper presentation]. College of Education, Criminal Justice, and Human Services (CECH) Spring Research Conference, University of Cincinnati, OH, United States.

Gay, G. (2000). *Culturally responsive teaching: Theory, research, & practice.* Teachers College Press.

Gay, G. (2018). *Culturally responsive teaching: Theory, research, and practice* (3rd ed.). Teachers College Press.

Gee, J. P. (2011). Discourse analysis: What makes it critical? In R. Rogers (Ed.), *An introduction to critical discourse analysis in education* (2nd ed., pp. 23–45). Routledge.

Gernsbacher, M. A. (2015). Video captions benefit everyone. *Policy Insights From the Behavioral and Brain Sciences, 2*(1), 195–202. https://doi.org/10.1177/2372732215602130

Glasgrow, N. A., & Hicks, C. D. (2009). *What successful teachers do: 101 research-based classroom strategies for new and veteran teachers.* Corwin Press.

Goldenberg, C. (1992–1993). Instructional conversations: Promoting comprehension through discussion. *The Reading Teacher, 46*(4), 316–326. https://www.jstor.org/stable/20201075

Goldman, S. E., & Burke, M. M. (2017). The effectiveness of interventions to increase parent involvement in special education: A systematic literature review and meta-analysis. *Exceptionality, 25*(2), 97–115. https://doi.org/10.1080/09362835.2016.1196444

Gonzalez-Barrero, A. M., & Nadig, A. S. (2017). Can bilingualism mitigate set-shifting difficulties in children with autism spectrum disorders? *Child Development, 90*(4), 1043–1060. https://doi.org/10.1111/cdev.12979

Greve, F. (2007, January 31). Curb ramps liberate Americans with disabilities—and everyone else. *McClatchy Newspapers.*

Gu, X., & Cai, H. (2019). How a semantic diagram tool influences transaction costs during collaborative problem solving. *Journal of Computer Assisted Learning, 35*(1), 23–33. https://doi.org/10.1111/jcal.12307

Gutiérrez, K., Rymes, B., & Larson, J. (1995). Script, counterscript, and underlife in the classroom: James Brown versus Brown v. Board of Education. *Harvard Educational Review, 65*(3), 445–471. https://doi.org/10.17763/haer.65.3.r16146n25h4mh384

Gutiérrez, K. D. (2008, April/May/June). Developing a sociocritical literacy in the third space. *Reading Research Quarterly, 43*(2), 148–164. https://doi.org/10.1598/RRQ.43.2.3

Gutiérrez, K. D., Baquedano-López, P., & Tejeda, C. (2003). Rethinking diversity: Hybridity and hybrid language practices in the third space. In S. Goodman, T. Lillis, J. Maybin, & N. Mercer (Eds.), Language, literacy, and education: A reader (pp. 171–187). The Open University.

Gutiérrez, K. D., Cortes, K., Cortez, A., DiGiacomo, D., Higgs, J., Johnson, P., Lizárraga, J. R., Mendoza, E., Tien, J., & Vakil, S. (2017). Replacing representation with imagination: Finding ingenuity in everyday practices. *Review of Research in Education, 41*(1), 30–60. https://doi.org/10.3102/0091732X16687523

Haft, S. L., Myers, C. A., & Hoeft, F. (2016). Socioemotional and cognitive resilience in children with reading disabilities. *Current Opinion in Behavioral Sciences, 10*, 133–141.

Hamayan, E., Marler, B., Sánchez-López, C., & Damico, J. (2013). *Special education considerations for English language learners: Delivering a continuum of services.* Caslon Publishing.

Hammond, Z. (2015). *Culturally responsive teaching and the brain: Promoting authentic engagement and rigor among culturally and linguistically diverse students.* Corwin.

Harry, B., & Klingner, J. K. (2014). *Why are so many minority students in special education? Understanding race & disability in schools* (2nd ed). Teachers College Press.

Hattie, J. A., & Donoghue, G. M. (2016). Learning strategies: A synthesis and conceptual model. *npj Science of Learning, 1*, article 16013. https://doi.org/10.1038/npjscilearn.2016.13

Haught, J. R., & McCafferty, S. G. (2008). Embodied language performance: Drama and the ZPD in the second language classroom. In J. P. Lantolf & M. E. Poehner (Eds.), *Sociocultural theory and the teaching of second languages* (pp. 139–162). Equinox.

Hernández Finch, M. E. (2012). Special considerations with response to intervention and instruction for students with diverse backgrounds. *Psychology in the Schools, 49*(3), 285–296. https://doi.org/10.1002/pits.21597

Herrera, S., & Murry, K. (2016). *Mastering ESL/EFL methods: Differentiated instruction for culturally and linguistically diverse (CLD) students* (3rd ed.). Pearson.

Herrera, S. G. (2010). *Biography-driven culturally responsive teaching.* Teachers College Press.

Herrera, S. G. (2016). *Biography-driven culturally responsive teaching* (2nd ed.). Teachers College Press.

Herrera, S. G. (2022). *Biography-driven culturally responsive teaching: Honoring race, ethnicity, and personal history* (3rd ed.). Teachers College Press.

Herrera, S. G., Cabral, R. M., & Murry, K. G. (2020). *Assessment of culturally and linguistically diverse students* (3rd ed.). Pearson.

Herrera, S. G., Kavimandan, S. K., & Holmes, M. A. (2011). *Crossing the vocabulary bridge: Differentiated strategies for diverse secondary classrooms.* Teachers College Press.

Herrera, S. G., Kavimandan, S. K., Perez, D. R., & Wessels, S. (2017). *Accelerating literacy for diverse learners: Classroom strategies that integrate social/emotional engagement and academic achievement, K–8* (2nd ed.). Teachers College Press.

Herrera, S. G., Porter, L., & Barko-Alva, K. (2020). *Equity in school–parent partnerships: Cultivating community and family trust in culturally diverse classrooms.* Teachers College Press.

Hoff, E. (2006). How social contexts support and shape language development. *Developmental Review, 26*(1), 55–88. https://doi.org/10.1016/j.dr.2005.11.002

Holmes, M. A. (2022). *Creating equitable spaces for all learners: Leveraging community expertise through situationally responsive instructional conversations* [Doctoral dissertation, Kansas State University]. K-State Research Exchange. https://hdl.handle.net/2097/42158

Hoover, J. J. (2012). Reducing unnecessary referrals. *Teaching Exceptional Children, 44*(4), 38–47. https://doi.org/10.1177/004005991204400404

Hoover, J. J., Erickson, J. R., Herron, S. R., & Smith, C. E. (2018). Implementing culturally and linguistically responsive special education eligibility assessment in rural county elementary schools: Pilot project. *Rural Special Education Quarterly, 37*(2), 90–102. https://doi.org/10.1177/8756870518761879

Hosp, J. L., & Reschly, D. J. (2004). Disproportionate representation of minority students in special education: Academic, demographic, and economic predictors. *Exceptional Children, 70*(2), 185–199. https://doi.org/10.1177/001440290407000204

Howe, M. J. A. (1999). *A teacher's guide to the psychology of learning* (2nd ed.). Blackwell.

Individuals With Disabilities Education Act (IDEA). (2004). Individuals With Disabilities Education Improvement Act of 2004, Pub. L. No. 108-446, §101. Retrieved November 1, 2022, from www.copyright.gov/legislation/pl108-446.pdf

Janssen, J., Kirschner, F., Erkens, G., Kirschner, P. A., & Paas, F. (2010). Making the black box of collaborative learning transparent: Combining process-oriented and cognitive load approaches. *Educational Psychology Review, 22*(2), 139–154. https://doi.org/10.1007/s10648-010-9131-x

Johnson, D. W., & Johnson, R. (1979). Conflict in the classroom: Controversy and learning. *Review of Educational Research, 49*(1), 51–70. https://doi.org/10.3102/00346543049001051

Johnson, D. W., & Johnson, R. (2007). *Creative controversy: Intellectual challenge in the classroom* (4th ed.). Interaction Book Company.

Johnson, D. W., Johnson, R., Roy, P., & Zaidman, B. (1985). Oral interaction in cooperative learning groups: Speaking, listening, and the nature of statements made by high-, medium-, and low-achieving students. *Journal of Psychology, 19*(4), 303–321. https://doi.org/10.1080/00223980.1985.9915450

Johnson, D. W., & Johnson, R. T. (1991). Collaboration and cognition. In A. L. Costa (Ed.), *Developing minds: A resource book for teaching thinking* (Rev. ed., Vol. 1, pp. 298–301). Association for Supervision and Curriculum Development. https://files.eric.ed.gov/fulltext/ED332166.pdf#page=310

Johnson, D. W., & Johnson, R. T. (2009). An educational psychology success story: Social interdependence theory and cooperative learning. *Educational Researcher, 38*(5), 365–379. https://doi.org/10.3102/0013189X09339057

Johnson, D. W., Johnson, R. T., & Holubec, E. J. (1991). *Cooperation in the classroom.* Interaction Book Company.

Jordan, C., Tharp, R. G., & Baird-Vogt, L. (2017). "Just open the door": Cultural compatibility and classroom rapport. In M. Saravia-Shore & S. F. Arvizu (Eds.), *Cross-cultural literacy: Ethnographies of communication in multiethnic classrooms* (pp. 3–18). Routledge.

Kangas, S. E. (2021). "Is it language or disability?": An ableist and monolingual filter for English learners with disabilities. *TESOL Quarterly, 55*(3), 673–683. https://doi.org/10.1002/tesq.3029

Klingner, J. K., Almanza, E., de Onis, C., & Barletta, L. M. (2008). *Misconceptions about the second language acquisition process.* Corwin.

Klingner, J. K., Artiles, A. J., Kozleski, E., Harry, B., Zion, S., Tate, W., Durán, G. Z., & Riley, D. (2005, September 8). Addressing the disproportionate representation of culturally and linguistically diverse students in special education through culturally responsive educational systems. *Education Policy Analysis Archives, 13*(38). https://www.redalyc.org/pdf/2750/275020513038.pdf

Klingner, J. K., & Harry, B. (2006). The special education referral and decision-making process for English language learners: Child study team meetings and placement conferences. *Teachers College Record, 108*(11), 2247–2281. https://doi.org/10.1111/j.1467-9620.2006.00781.x

Klingner, J. K., & Vaughn, S. (2002). The changing roles and responsibilities of an LD specialist. *Learning Disability Quarterly, 25,* 19–31. https://doi.org/10.2307/1511188

Kolano, L. Q., Dávila, L. T., Lachance, J., & Coffey, H. (2014). Multicultural teacher education: Why teachers say it matters in preparing them for English language learners. *CATESOL Journal, 25*(1), 41–65. https://files.eric.ed.gov/fulltext/EJ1111871.pdf

Kothari, B., & Takeda, J. (2000). Same language subtitling for literacy: Small change for colossal gains. In S. C. Bhatnagar & R. Schware (Eds.), *Information and communication technology in development* (pp. 176–186). SAGE.

Krashen, S. D. (1982). *Principles and practice in second language acquisition.* Pergamon Press.

Krashen, S. D. (2005). Bilingual education and second language acquisition theory. In C. F. Leyba, *Schooling and language minority students: A theoretico-practical framework* (3rd ed., pp. 47–75). Legal Books. (Original work published 1984)

Ladson-Billings, G. (1994). *The dreamkeepers: Successful teachers of African American children.* Jossey Bass.

Lantolf, J. P., & Poehner, M. E. (2008). Introduction. In J. P. Lantolf & M. E. Poehner (Eds.), *Sociocultural theory and the teaching of second languages* (pp. 1–30). Equinox.

LeBarton, E. S., Goldin-Meadow, S., & Raudenbush, S. (2015). Experimentally induced increases in early gesture lead to increases in spoken vocabulary. *Journal of Cognition and Development, 16*(2), 199–220. https://doi.org/10.1080/15248372.2013.858041

Linebarger, D., Piotrowski, J. T., & Greenwood, C. R. (2010). On screen print: The role of captions as a supplemental literacy tool. *Journal of Research in Reading, 33*(2), 148–167. https://doi.org/10.1111/j.1467-9817.2009.01407.x

MacDonald, G. L., Miller, S. S., Murry, K., Herrera, S., & Spears, J. D. (2013). Efficacy of ACA strategies in biography-driven science teaching: An investigation. *Cultural Studies in Science Education, 3*(8), 889–903. https://doi.org/10.1007/s11422-013-9517-4

Madler, A. M., Anderson, S. K., LeMire, S. D., & Smith, K. (2022). Perceptions of teacher preparation for class room diversity. *Mid-Western Educational Researcher, 34*(1), 42–68. https://www.mwera.org/MWER/volumes/v34/issue1/MWER-V34n1-Madler-FEATURE-ARTICLE.pdf

Maki, K. E., & Adams, S. R. (2020). Special education evaluation practices and procedures: Implications for referral and eligibility decision-making. *Contemporary School Psychology, 26*, 350–358. https://doi.org/10.1007/s40688-020-00335-4

Maldonado, J. A. (1994). Bilingual special education: Specific learning disabilities in language and reading. *Journal of Education Issues of Language Minority Students, 14*(2), 127–147. https://ncela.ed.gov/files/rcd/BE020253/Bilingual_Special_Education.pdf

Marr y Ortega, L. (2022). *Transforming teacher perspectives of culturally and linguistically diverse families through critical reflection* [Doctoral dissertation, Kansas State University]. K-State Research Exchange. https://hdl.handle.net/2097/42183

Matias, C. E., & Mackey, J. (2016). Breakin' down whiteness in antiracist teaching: Introducing critical whiteness pedagogy. *The Urban Review, 48*(1), 32–50. https://doi.org/10.1007/s11256-015-0344-7

Mellom, P. J., Hixon, R. K., & Weber, J. P. (2019). *With a little help from my friends: Conversation-based instruction for culturally and linguistically diverse (CLD) classrooms.* Teachers College Press.

Moll, L. C., Amanti, C., Neff, D., & González, N. (1992). Funds of knowledge for teaching: Using a qualitative approach to connect homes and classrooms. *Theory into Practice, 31*(2), 132–141.

Montalvo, R., Combes, B., & Kea, C. (2014). Perspectives on culturally and linguistically responsive RtI pedagogics through a cultural and linguistic lens. *Interdisciplinary Journal of Teaching and Learning, 4*(3), 203–211.

Morgan, H. (2020). Misunderstood and mistreated: Students of color in special education. *Voices of Reform, 3*(2), 71–81. https://doi.org/10.32623/3.10005

Morris, K. K., Frechette, C., Dukes, L., III, Stowell, N., Topping, N. E., & Brodosi, D. (2016). Closed captioning matters: Examining the value of closed captions for "all" students. *Journal of Postsecondary Education and Disability, 29*(3), 231–238. https://eric.ed.gov/?id=EJ1123786

National Center for Education Statistics (NCES). (2020). *Digest of education statistics.* U.S. Department of Education, Institute of Education Sciences. https://nces.ed.gov/programs/digest/d20/tables/dt20_209.42.asp

National Center for Education Statistics (NCES). (2021). *Digest of education statistics.* U.S. Department of Education, Institute of Education Sciences. https://nces.ed.gov/programs/digest/d21/tables/dt21_204.20.asp

National Center for Education Statistics (NCES). (2022). English learners in public schools. *Condition of education.* U.S. Department of Education, Institute of Education Sciences. https://nces.ed.gov/programs/coe/indicator/cgf

National Center for Learning Disabilities. (2020). *Significant disproportionality in special education: Trends among English learners (ELs).* https://www.ncld.org/wp-content/uploads/2020/10/2020-NCLD-Disproportionality_-English-Learners_EL_FINAL.pdf

National Center on Response to Intervention (NCRTI). (2010). *Essential components of RTI—A closer look at response to intervention.* https://files.eric.ed.gov/fulltext/ED526858.pdf

National Reading Panel (US), National Institute of Child Health, Human Development (US), National Reading Excellence Initiative, National Institute for Literacy (US), United States Public Health Service, & United States Department of Health. (2000). *Report of the National Reading Panel: Teaching children to read: An evidence-based assessment of the scientific research literature on reading and its implications for reading instruction: Reports of the subgroups.* National Institute of Child Health and Human Development, National Institutes of Health.

Nganga, L. (2015). Culturally responsive and anti-biased teaching benefits early childhood pre-service teachers. *Journal of Curriculum and Teaching, 4*(2), 1–16.

Nieto, S. (1992). *Affirming diversity: The sociopolitical context of multicultural education.* Longman.

Office of English Language Acquisition. (2020, February). *English learners: Demographic trends.* https://ncela.ed.gov/files/fast_facts/19-0193_Del4.4_ELDemographicTrends_021220_508.pdf

Ormrod, J. E. (1995). *Human learning* (2nd ed.). Prentice Hall.

Orosco, M. J., & Klingner, J. (2010). One school's implementation of RTI with English language learners: "Referring into RTI." *Journal of Learning Disabilities, 43*(3), 269–288. https://doi.org/10.1177/0022219409355474

Paris, D. (2012). Culturally sustaining pedagogy: A needed change in stance, terminology, and practice. *Educational Researcher, 41*(3), 93–97. https://doi.org/10.3102/0013189X12441244

Peña, E., Iglesias, A., & Lidz, C. S. (2001). Reducing test bias through dynamic assessment of children's word learning ability. *American Journal of Speech-Language Pathology, 10*(2), 138–154. https://doi.org/10.1044/1058-0360(2001/014)

Pérez, D., Holmes, M., Miller, S., & Fanning, C. (2012). Biography-driven strategies as the great equalizer: Universal conditions that promote K–12 culturally responsive teaching. *Journal of Curriculum and Instruction, 6*(1), 25–42. https://doi.org/10.3776/joci.2012.v6n1p25-42

Pontier, R., & Gort, M. (2016). Coordinated translanguaging pedagogy as distributed cognition: A case study of two dual language bilingual education preschool coteachers' languaging practices during shared book readings. *International Multilingual Research Journal, 10*(2), 89–106. https://doi.org/10.1080/19313152.2016.1150732

Porter, L. (2018). Journeying together/Compañeros de camino: Improving parent relations within dual-language immersion programs as a model for cross-cultural understanding and collaboration. *Journal of Interdisciplinary Studies in Education, 6*(2), 19–31. https://ojed.org/index.php/jise/article/view/1428

Pratt-Johnson, Y. (2006). Communicating cross-culturally: What teachers should know. *The Internet TESL Journal, 12*(2), 5. http://iteslj.org/Articles/Pratt-Johnson-CrossCultural

Resnick, L. B., Michaels, S., & O'Connor, M. C. (2010). How (well-structured) talk builds the mind. In D. D. Preiss & R. J. Sternberg (Eds.), *Innovations in educational psychology: Perspectives on learning, teaching, and human development* (pp. 163–194). Springer Publishing Company.

Reyes, N. M. (2022). *An exploration of general education teachers' perceptions of culturally and linguistically diverse (CLD) students during a general education intervention (GEI) process* [Doctoral dissertation, Kansas State University]. K-State Research Exchange. https://hdl.handle.net/2097/42207

Reyes, N., & Steen, L. H., II. (2021). *Sources of data for culturally-linguistically diverse students in the general education intervention process.* Unpublished manuscript.

Rhodes, R., Ochoa, S. H., & Ortiz, S. O. (2005). *Comprehensive assessment of culturally and linguistically diverse students: A practical approach.* Guilford.

Rodríguez, A., & Rodríguez, D. (2017). English learners with learning disabilities: What is the current state? *Insights Into Learning Disabilities, 14*(1), 97–112.

Rodriguez, E. R., Bellanca, J. A., & Esparza, D. R. (2017). *What is it about me you can't teach: Culturally responsive instruction in deeper learning classrooms.* Corwin Press.

Ruiz, N. T. (1989). An optimal learning environment for Rosemary. *Exceptional Children, 56*(2), 130–144. https://doi.org/10.1177/001440298905600205

Saleebey, D. (2001). *Human behavior and social environments: A biopsychosocial approach.* Columbia University Press.

Sedova, K., Salamounova, Z., & Svaricek, R. (2014). Troubles with dialogic teaching. *Learning, Culture and Social Interaction, 3*(4), 274–285. https://doi.org/10.1016/j.lcsi.2014.04.001

Skiba, R. J., Simmons, A. B., Ritter, S., Gibb, A. C., Rausch, M. K., Cuadrado, J., & Chung, C.-G. (2008). Achieving equity in special education: History, status, and current challenges. *Exceptional Children, 7*(3), 264–288. https://doi.org/10.1177/001440290807400301

Sousa, D. A. (2017). *How the brain learns* (5th ed.). Corwin Press.

Staal, M. A., Bolton, A. E., Yaroush, R. A., & Bourne, L. E., Jr. (2008). Cognitive performance and resilience to stress. In B. J. Lukey & V. Tepe (Eds.), *Biobehavioral resilience to stress* (pp. 259–299). Routledge. https://doi.org/10.1201/9781420071788

Steen, L. (2022). *Whiteness: Influence, decision-making, and cultural-linguistic disproportionality in special education placements* [Doctoral dissertation, Kansas State University]. K-State Research Exchange. https://hdl.handle.net/2097/42081

Sullivan, A. L. (2011). Disproportionality in special education identification and placement of English language learners. *Exceptional Children, 77*(3), 317–334. https://doi.org/10.1177/001440291107700304

Symeou, L., & Karagiorgi, Y. (2018). Culturally aware but not yet ready to teach the "others": Reflections on a Roma education teacher training programme. *Journal for Multicultural Education, 12*(4), 314–329. http://dx.doi.org/10.1108/JME-02-2017-0012

Thomas, W. P., & Collier, V. P. (1997). *School effectiveness for language minority students* (NCBE Resource Collection Series No. 9). National Clearinghouse for Bilingual Education. https://eric.ed.gov/?id=ED436087

Thomas, W. P., & Collier, V. P. (2002). *A national study of school effectiveness for language minority students' long-term academic achievement.* Center for Research on Education, Diversity & Excellence, University California–Santa Cruz. https://eric.ed.gov/?id=ed475048

Thordardottir, E. (2010). Towards evidence-based practice in language intervention for bilingual children. *Journal of Communication Disorders, 43*(6), 523–537. https://doi.org/10.1016/j.jcomdis.2010.06.001

Title VI of the Civil Rights Act of 1964, 42 U.S.C. § 2000d, *et seq.* https://www.justice.gov/crt/fcs/TitleVI-Overview

Torres, C., & Rao, C. (2019). *UDL for language learners.* CAST Professional Publishing.

Turkle, S. (2017). *Alone together: Why we expect more from technology and less from each other* (Rev. ed.). Basic Books.

U.S. Department of Education. (2002). *Twenty-fourth annual report to Congress on the implementation of the Individuals With Disabilities Education Act.* Retrieved November 9, 2022, from www.ed.gov/about/offices/list/osers/osep/research.html

Valenzuela, A. (1999). *Subtractive schooling: U.S.-Mexican youth and the politics of caring.* State University of New York Press.

Vanderplank, R. (2016). *Captioned media in foreign language learning and teaching: Subtitles for the deaf and hard-of-hearing as tools for language learning.* Springer.

van Lier, L. (2004). *The ecology and semiotics of language learning: A socio-cultural perspective.* Kluwer Academic Publishers.

Voulgarides, C. K. (2018). *Does compliance matter in special education? IDEA and the hidden inequities of practice.* Teachers College Press.

Vygotsky, L. S. (1978). *Mind in society: The development of higher psychological processes* (M. Cole, V. John-Steiner, S. Scribner, & E. Souberman, Eds. & Trans.). Harvard University Press.

Waitoller, F. R., Artiles, A. J., & Cheney, D. A. (2010). The miner's canary: A review of overrepresentation research and explanations. *The Journal of Special Education, 44*(1), 29–49. https://doi.org/10.1177/0022466908329226

Walqui, A., & van Lier, L. (2010). *Scaffolding the academic success of adolescent English language learners: A pedagogy of promise.* WestEd.

Walton, P. H., Baca, L., & Escamilla, K. (2005). *A national study of teacher education preparation for diverse student populations.* Center for Research on Education, Diversity and Excellence.

Weinstein, Y. (2017, April 13). *How long is short-term memory? Shorter than you might think.* The Learning Scientists. https://www.learningscientists.org/blog/2017/4/13-1?rq=How%20long%20is%20short-term%20memory%3F%20Shorter%20than%20you%20might%20think

Wilkerson, C., & Ortiz, A. (1986). *Characteristics of limited English proficient and English proficient learning disabled Hispanic students at initial assessment and at reevaluation.* University of Texas, Department of Special Education, Handicapped Minority Research Institute. https://eric.ed.gov/?id=ED283314

Wormeli, R. (n.d.). *Key to motivation: Student agency.* Association for Middle Level Education. https://www.amle.org/key-to-motivation-student-agency/

Index

About the Authors

SOCORRO G. HERRERA is a professor in the Department of Curriculum and Instruction, College of Education at Kansas State University and serves as the Executive Director of the Center for Intercultural and Multilingual Advocacy (CIMA). She is certified in elementary education, bilingual education, and school counseling. As an international keynote speaker, district consultant, and trainer of trainers, she has collaborated with teachers across the country and the world to chart new paths to academic success for culturally and linguistically diverse (CLD) learners. Her research focuses on the role that personal histories of the learner, family, and teacher play in literacy development and culturally responsive, sustaining pedagogy; reading strategies; and teacher preparation for diverse classrooms. Dr. Herrera has authored nine textbooks and numerous articles for publication in journals such as *Bilingual Research Journal*, *Journal of Hispanic Higher Education*, *Journal of Research in Education*, *Journal of Latinos and Education*, *Journal of Curriculum and Instruction*, *International Journal of Multicultural Education*, *Teacher Education Quarterly*, and *Urban Education*.

DIANE RODRÍGUEZ is a professor and serves as an associate dean at Fordham University, Graduate School of Education. Her research is at the intersection of special education and bilingual education. Dr. Rodríguez has been an invited speaker at national and international conferences on special education and bilingual education. Univision selected Dr. Rodríguez as an example of "Orgullo de Nuestra Comunidad," which highlights individuals who give back to the community. She was recognized for her work with individuals with disabilities. Dr. Rodríguez is the founder of Every Girl Is Important, a not-for-profit organization to educate and empower young girls. For more information: www.everygirlisimportant.org. She is the coauthor of *The Bilingual Advantage*, a book published by Teachers College Press. Dr. Rodríguez has authored articles for numerous nationally known journals, such as *Exceptional Children*, *Journal of Hispanic Higher Education*, *International Journal of Bilingual Education and Bilingualism*, *Insights into Learning Disabilities*, *Journal of Multilingual Education Research*, and *Learning Disabilities Research & Practice*.

ROBIN M. CABRAL is an educational consultant with a background in district-level administration, bilingual speech-language pathology, special education (SPED), literacy, assessment, and intervention development for culturally and linguistically diverse (CLD) students. Dr. Cabral's consulting activities emphasize scientifically grounded, educator-accessible practices to ensure the full access of CLD and SPED students to an inviting, affirming, and enriching curriculum with appropriately individualized supports. Dr. Cabral has coauthored two books: *Assessment of Culturally and Linguistically Diverse Students* (3rd ed.) (2020) and *Assessment Accommodations for Classroom Teachers of Culturally and Linguistically Diverse Students* (2nd ed.) (2013).

MELISSA A. HOLMES is associate director of the Center for Intercultural and Multilingual Advocacy (CIMA) in the College of Education at Kansas State University. Her teaching, research, and professional development efforts with K–12 educators emphasize capacity building for culturally responsive and sustaining teaching, literacy and language development, and applications of biography-driven instruction in U.S. and international K–12 settings. Dr. Holmes has coauthored *Crossing the Vocabulary Bridge: Differentiated Strategies in Diverse Secondary Classrooms* (2011) with Teachers College Press. She also has authored numerous book chapters and articles in journals such as *American Secondary Education*, *Forum for International Research in Education*, *Journal of Bilingual Educational Research and Instruction*, *Journal of Curriculum and Instruction*, *Journal of Multicultural Education*, *Multicultural Learning and Teaching*, *Teaching Education*, and *Teaching Education Quarterly*.